A MIRROR FOR FOOLS

THE BOOK OF BURNEL THE ASS

by

NIGEL LONGCHAMP

of the Benedictine Priory of
Christchurch, Canterbury
(ca. 1180)

TRANSLATED FROM THE LATIN BY

J. H. MOZLEY

WITH ILLUSTRATIONS BY

EVE GRAHAM

AND A PREFACE BY

PAUL E. BEICHNER, C.S.C.

UNIVERSITY OF NOTRE DAME PRESS

University of Notre Dame Press
Notre Dame, Indiana

First paperback edition, January 1963

First published in Great Britain in 1961 by
B. H. BLACKWELL, LTD., OXFORD

MANUFACTURED IN THE UNITED STATES OF AMERICA

PREFACE TO THE AMERICAN EDITION

If one excludes the whimsical cartoons of monks, little Sisters, choirboys and servers, and the like, which are intended for brief moments of mild amusement, there is very little clerical, monastic or ecclesiastical humor published in the United States today. Clerical jokes and anecdotes are transmitted orally, and some may receive wide circulation, such as the quip attributed to Pope John. When he was asked the question: "How many people work at the Vatican?" he answered: "About half of them." Satirical pieces are more rare, but occasionally one is composed and circulated privately among clerics and religious who are friends. A recent example is the "New Rubrics for the Recitation of the Rosary," which is a burlesque of the new rubrics for the recitation of the Office. It was written by an ecclesiastic for ecclesiastics who reverence the Office as liturgical prayer, but who are irked by the directions for minute changes. The spirit of it is like that of many medieval satirical pieces; the critical attitude is indeed there and the laughter elicited is intended not to tear down but to bring about improvement. Had it been written in the Middle Ages, it might have found its way into the *Carmina Burana,* or a similar collection.

There is still laughter today among ecclesiastics and professional religious in monasteries, religious houses, rectories, and convents, and for them the step backwards to the clerical humor of the Middle Ages, such as much of that in *A Mirror for Fools,* is a short one. For the layman or the person unfamiliar with current ecclesiastical functionaries and institutions, the step is a longer one. Satire is

iii

not an unsophisticated type of literature. The enjoyment of satire, medieval or modern, involving irony, parody, or burlesque requires knowledge, just as the enjoyment of a television imitation of a celebrity requires that the celebrity be recognized. A second requirement is a humane tolerance, amused detachment, and ability to laugh at human aberrations, wherever they are found. The enjoyment of clerical or ecclesiastical satire has a third requirement — a sound faith, secure in knowledge and the foundations of belief. The timorous or religiously insecure person tends to see blasphemy where none was intended or none exists; he cannot understand how God's children can sometimes play like children in their Father's house. The pietistic person fails to see anything funny in deviations from the solemn; perhaps because his religion has already passed over into religiosity, he is too easily scandalized. The safety valve of laughter is important for everyone, and it should not be tied down by taking fun seriously, even though fun may contain a serious point.

A Mirror for Fools was written in Latin verse by a Benedictine monk and priest chiefly for a clerical audience nearly eight centuries ago, but we believe that an English translation will be enjoyed not just by students of medieval literature but also by clergy and laity alike. If a reader cares to look obliquely into the *Mirror,* he will see the images and reflections somehow changing before his eyes into quite modern characters, functionaries, institutions, and situations. Human frailties, vanities, and foibles are recognizable in any dress because they are human. The author, Nigel Longchamp, as an urbane humanist of the cloister acquainted with the world of affairs, wrote this enduring little classic; J. H. Mozley, emeritus Reader of Latin in the University of London, has translated it with spirit and grace; and Eve Graham has given the edition added charm with her illustrations.

It is no secret that the hero of *A Mirror for Fools,* Burnel the Ass, represents a monk or any ecclesiastic who is dissatisfied with his lot and who vainly wishes to become a prior, an abbot, or a bishop. Nigel makes the point clear in his prose preface that Burnel searching for the means of acquiring a longer and more luxuriant tail is such a person in search of preferment. But because Burnel is a likeable character, even if he is an ass, a reader willingly goes along with him on his adventures, from Cremona where he had escaped from his master, to Salerno, to Lyons and Paris, and back to Cremona again, still an inveterate optimistic dreamer. But this is only the framework into which Nigel has poured a number of time-tested fables, a picture of student life at Paris, a satirical view of the Religious Orders, a general satire on the Roman Curia, bishops and pastors, abbots and priors, on princes and all classes of lay society, on venality and the almighty power of money. Here is plenty indeed.

A word might be said about the review of the Religious Orders. After Burnel has succeeded in losing to dogs half of the tail which nature had given him, and after he has failed to learn anything at the schools of Paris — even French — he decides to enter the religious life. Thereupon he reviews the existing Orders, mixing approved and commendable details of rule and fact with gossip and sly insinuations of laxity. Finally convinced that none would be quite satisfactory to his tastes, he decides to found his own Order, whose Rule will exclude the particular austerities practiced by any one of the existing Orders but will include the concessions which each Order had made in view of the work or the way of life of its members. Thus, in Burnel's Rule the innuendoes and insinuations of laxity in the previous descriptions are collected and re-emphasized. Like the Black Canons, Burnel and his followers will eat meat; like the Templars, they will travel on horseback; like the Hospitallers, who seem to indulge in lying to magnify the House, they will lie at will.

> This from the Hospital would I retain,
> Where'er I am to lie with might and main.

A review of the later Mendicant Orders was interpolated in four manuscripts; it may be found in an appendix to the Latin edition of the poem (*Speculum Stultorum,* eds. John H. Mozley and Robert R. Raymo, University of California Press, 1960). But to my knowledge, no one has attempted to review in similar satirical fashion the Religious Orders or Congregations founded since the Middle Ages.

A Mirror for Fools proved to be quite popular in the late Middle Ages, even though its topic was somewhat limited. Forty manuscripts of the poem still exist. This is twice the number of extant manuscripts of Chaucer's *Troilus and Criseyde* and nearly half the number of manuscripts of *The Canterbury Tales.* From the beginning, writers mined the *Mirror* for anecdotes and illustrations, for proverbial sayings, ready-made lines, and satirical ammunition. Chaucer used the story of the revenge of the injured cock in "The Nun's Priest's Tale," itself a mock-heroic beast-fable told by a character of wit and wisdom, a humanist of the cloister, not unlike the creator of Burnel the Ass.

To read *A Mirror for Fools* as though Nigel were bent on tearing down institutions — monasticism, the Church, the State — is to misread the poem. Nigel believed in them. He also believed that people of all positions should be better, and that they would be better if they learned caution from the mistakes of others. But like Burnel the Ass, a man who seeks foolishness always remains what he was before:

> Burnello teste, qui, dum quaesivit inepta,
> Semper permansit quod prius ipse fuit.

Paul E. Beichner, C.S.C.

University of Notre Dame

INTRODUCTION
CHARACTERS OF THE POEM

BURNEL.....................a runaway Ass from Cremona

GALEN.....................,.................................his doctor

BRUNETTA and BICORNIS....a wise and a foolish heifer
(in Galen's Tale)

A LONDON MERCHANT........doing business in Salerno

FROMUND..............a Cistercian lay-brother, near Lyons

ARNOLD.....................a fellow-wayfarer with Burnel

GUNDULF.................the young son of a country priest
(in Arnold's Tale)

A COCK, and COPPA, a Hen.............(in Arnold's Tale)

A RAVEN, a COCK and a HAWK......(in the Parliament
of Birds)

THREE GODDESSES............(in Burnel's Bother's Tale)

BERNARD.............................Burnel's old master

DRYANE...................................a rich Lord

SUMMARY OF THE POEM

Author's Prologue. Dedication to William. His verses are weak, but contain truth. Time brings changes, and circumstances brings out differences. The young often claim the wisdom of their elders, and a fair exterior may hide weakness within. An Ass in a lion's skin will sooner or later be shown for what he is.

An Ass wishes to get a longer tail, and consults Galen; his advice.

His story of the two cows, Brunetta and Bicornis.

Further advice; he sends Burnel off to Salerno with a mock recipe for tail-lengthening.

Burnel arrives at Salerno; his encounter with the Merchant there.

He leaves Salerno and returns by the Rhone.

He is attacked by Fromund's dogs, and suffers the loss of half his tail; he pretends to be the Papal Legate, and takes revenge on Fromund.

He decides to go to Paris, and become a Master in the Schools; on the way he meets Arnold, a Sicilian.

Arnold's story of the Cockerel's revenge.

The English students in Paris; Burnel's gloomy reflections on his failure there.

He dreams of becoming a Bishop; story of how he once rescued the Mayor of his town, and the Mayor's ingratitude.

He leaves Paris, but finds he has forgotten its name. An encounter with a pilgrim recovers the name, but he loses it again except for the first syllable. Discouraged, he decides to enter the religious life.

Review of the existing Orders; he determines to found a new one that will contain all the best points of the rest.

Burnel meets Galen, and explains his purpose; he bewails the corruptions of Rome and the Church. His strictures on lay society are veiled under the form of a fable, in which he relates a discussion held by birds overheard by him.

He urges Galen to join him in the life of religion; if Galen will have to become subordinate to Burnel, life is full of such misfits; he tells the story of the Three Goddesses to illustrate it.

A sudden nose-bleed causes Burnel to augur some ill chance. Suddenly his old master Bernard enters the inn where he has been talking to Galen, and takes him off home again, still dreaming of some glorious destiny in the future.

The story of Bernard and the Three Grateful Beasts.

Author's Epilogue. He points the moral of the story of Burnel, the retribution which ingratitude often meets, the dangers of ambitious projects that have no hope of fulfilment. Happy he who can learn from the fate of others.

COMMENT

Nigel has here written an animal fable in order to satirize certain aspects of monastic life. First there is the restlessness and discontent which makes the inmate of a cloister try to get free by seeking occupation in the outer world, though at imminent peril to his soul; he would like to study in the Schools and rise to a Mastership, or become a bishop, or even obtain a small administrative post in his Order. Next, he satirizes the tendency to multiply Orders by giving humorous descriptions of the many different institutions of his time, laying chief stress on what is worn and what is eaten, but finding opportunity to indulge his dislikes, particularly of the Cistercians for their land-grabbing ways, and of Secular Canons for their dangerous compromise with the world, and also because of the threat to replace the Benedictines of Canterbury with a College of such Canons. More generally, the work is intended as a warning against foolishness in living; hence its title, "A Mirror for Fools," in which wise men look and take warning, and fools can see themselves for what they are.

Nigel's poem is characteristic of his age. Satire in various forms flourished in the lively civilisation of the twelfth and thirteenth centuries, in which there was constant intercourse between the centres of population. Criticism of abuses was vented in direct, often personal attacks, though sometimes veiled under the form of animal fables, a literary type of immemorial ancestry, springing from the short apologue as we find it in Aesop or Phaedrus, and often developed in longer poems.

The tenth century, for instance, produced a fable called *The Captive's Escape,* in which a calf escapes from his mother's care, and is in danger of falling victim to a wolf; other animals, fox, hedgehog and otter, take his part, and he is saved from destruction. Here is Nigel's own theme, for the calf typifies the straying monk who ventures into the perils of the world. The theme of Wolf and Fox, better known to later times as *Reynard the Fox* is found in a long poem full of allegory and satire called *Ysengrimus.* The ass himself is found first in a short fable about the Ass in a Lion's skin, another germ of nucleus from which our poem has developed, for the lion's skin is here replaced by the professor's gown or the bishop's robe of which Burnel dreams so hopelessly. Another poem which has, as it were, evolved from a popular proverb is the *Asinarius,* a kind of fairy story in which a king and queen have an ass born to them, he becomes an expert player of the lyre (the proverb is "asinus lyram," denoting the impossibility of an ass playing on the lyre), marries a princess, and at night sheds his skin and becomes a handsome prince. Finally, we cannot think of Burnel wandering on the roads of the world without recalling the famous *Golden Ass* of Apuleius, well-known in the Middle Ages, in which the ass does not, as with Nigel, typify a human being, but is a real man magically transformed into an ass. Whereas the earlier apologue has only animals talking and acting with each other (as in the *Captive's Escape*), in the later forms, as in the *Golden Ass* and in our poem, he has only to do with human beings and behaves to them as one.

The medieval writers were great story-tellers, and looked back to Ovid as their exemplar. By the twelfth and thirteenth centuries the poets had acquired much of his story-telling craft; his verse came to be the model in the schools, and something like his facility and genial flow is found in the poets of the time. Nigel has much of this, though he is too much given to the medieval tendency to moralize, and also to a redundancy of style that calls for occasional pruning. He has learnt how to interpose stories to fit them into his narrative. As the thirteenth century went on, the vernacular languages take over from the Latin; Nigel may be regarded as a link between Ovid and Chaucer, who refers to one of the stories in this work, the *Cockerel's Revenge,* in his *Nun's Priest's Tale* (*CT,* VII, 3312-3316; B, 4502-4506):

> I have wel rad in 'Daun Burnel the Asse,'
> Among his vers, how that ther was a cok,
> For that a preestes sone yaf hym a knok
> Upon his leg whil he was yong and nyce,
> He made hym for to lese his benefice.

It is clear that Nigel liked writing about animals, which are indeed everywhere in his poem, in references, proverbs and quotations. The black and white of the Augustinians' robe reminds him of magpie or leopard, and he can produce a formidable list of omens drawn from animals, such as hare, goat, toad and owl.

Others are used to exemplify the hypocrisy of those who profess to have denounced the world, but use that profession to get more than their due share of it. There is a Chaucerian character about the Cock and his mate, while in the "Parliament" the birds are well portrayed, the gloomy and censorious raven, the jaunty, self-satisfied cock and the aristocratic hawk. The ass himself has a character of his own; tricked and bullied, cast down to despair after each failure, he yet rises superior to misfortune, undefeatable in his assurance that in the end a glorious destiny awaits him; he humbly accepts the doctor's admonitions, yet he persists in his purpose, is unaffectedly glad to meet him again, and then with a delicious naivety exhorts him to join him in the religious life, even though it mean that the doctor must humble himself before Burnel as his religious superior.

The human characters are comparatively few; Galen the doctor combines sensible advice with chaff to turn the ass from his folly, but humours him when he finds him obstinate. Bernard, the typical rustic, shows a grim humour when he recovers the runaway, cropping his ears "that the cautery may teach him caution." In the final tale he is honest and superstitious, but too eager for money to let superstitious fears prevail. The London Merchant and Fromund are both well drawn, the former in the blend of solemnity and insolence with which he tricks the ass, the latter in the raucous vulgarity of the bully and coward.

Parody is a frequent element in medieval Satire, and was often carried to extremes of impudence. Nigel contents himself with poking fun at the solemnities of medicine, philosophy and law, and with parodying (if that is not too strong a term here) some well-known hymns; Brunetta, in the gravity of her admonitions, and Burnel himself in his song of triumph, are instances of this. His Review of the Orders, too, in its deliberate concentration on details of food and clothing, is in the nature of parody.

It will be seen that Nigel's method varies from direct attack and continuous invective to the veiled satire of the narrative or of the romantic fable, as seen in the "Parliament." There is also allegory in the stories incorporated in the narrative; for instance, the two cows are intended to show the different ways in which cloister monks react to hardships or to the call of kindred, how far they keep their eternal salvation before their eyes, or succumb to the world and the attacks of the devil and his imps. The revenge taken by the cock illustrates the evils of the unforgiving spirit. One can also trace the triple interpretation dear to the medieval mind: the literal meaning, the limited application (to the discontented monk), and the general significance, that is a warning to all those who set their affections on things below rather than on things above.

Little is known of the Author himself. I have given him the name of Longchamp, because it is found in the title of a miscellaneous collection of his poems (Nigelli de Longo Campo). The MS may indeed be an autograph, which gives a special authority to the name. It would imply either that he was born at Longchamp in Normandy, or, what is more likely, that he was a kinsman (he would be a slightly older contemporary) of William Longchamp, who was Chancellor under Richard I. Nigel's father, however, was Gilbert de Sarneis, that is, of Guernsey, and his sister, Agatha de Sarneis, rented property in Canterbury. The name given Nigel by John Bale (1493-1562), Wireker, is now considered mistaken; it probably arose from a misreading of the name Weteker, i.e. Whitacre, a small hamlet near Canterbury, in a manuscript containing verses attributed to Nigel. In none of the MSS of this poem, however, is Nigel given any surname at all. Surnames, in fact, were not at this period firmly established as belonging to the individual.

Nigel had joined the Benedictine Priory of Christchurch, Canterbury, before 1170, since he refers to himself elsewhere as having personally known the Archbishop, Thomas Becket, who was murdered in that year. We know that Nigel accompanied a deputation from the Priory to plead its cause at Rome in a dispute with Henry II and Archbishop Baldwin. He was a scholar of wide learning, well read in the Latin Classics and in the abundant literature of his time, and showing the skill in versification which characterizes the age. *A Mirror for Fools* was probably written between 1179 and 1180, with some later editions. Nigel was born perhaps about 1130, and may have survived into the following century.

TRANSLATOR'S PREFACE

Though Nigel's poem is written throughout in Latin Elegiacs I have preferred to vary the metre, and, while keeping in the main to rhymed couplets of either eight or ten syllables, have sometimes used alternate rhyming lines. Two of the sections, those of the Parliament of Birds and the Three Goddesses, I have tried to render in stanza form, and in one isolated case, Burnel's Song of Triumph, I have used a different metre altogether.

In some passages Nigel's redundancies of expression have needed a certain amount of pruning. This redundancy was a fault of the time, and was encouraged rather than checked by the schools in which Latin Verse Composition was taught. In two cases I have omitted an entire passage; for these see the Notes on pp. 109, 113.

Nigel is much given to punning; some of his puns do not go easily into English, and I have had to ignore them; elsewhere I have tried to reproduce the play on words.

For information in the Introduction and Notes I have used the recent edition of the original by myself and Robert R. Raymo (University of California Press, Berkeley and Los Angeles, 1960). I have included in the Notes only so much as seems necessary for the understanding of the allusions.

A MIRROR FOR FOOLS

To William, his beloved and ever to be beloved brother in Christ, his own Nigel—greeting in the Saviour's name! I sent thee of late a book whose text and title appear ridiculous to those who read and understand not; yet if thou wilt examine all with carefulness and pay attention to the writer's mind and purpose, though his style be as rude as his matter thou wilt in some degree be instructed. Wherefore in order that what is veiled beneath dissembling words may come forth for thee into the light, I have thought it right to lay bare for thee something of my riddlings. The title then of this book is as followeth: "A Mirror for Fools," which is so named for this purpose, that the witless beholding the folly of others may have it for a mirror, whereby to correct their own, and may learn that that is to be reprehended in themselves which they see as in a mirror to be reprehensible in others. But even as a mirror presents to those who gaze at it their form and feature, yet in no way preserves in their minds the memory of the presentment once it is past, so too with fools is it wont to be rare, yea difficult, that they be recalled from their own folly, howe'ersomuch they be instructed by that of others. 'Tis called therefore "A Mirror for Fools," either because fools, having beheld wisdom straightway forget it, or because the wise take advantage from this too, namely that from regarding the stupidity of fools they dispose themselves aright, and from seeing the beam in another's eye they cast out the mote from their own.

Dear William, half, and more, of my own heart,
Accept from your old Nigel in good part
These few poor lines penned lately by his hand;
And take it not amiss that as they stand
The subject's rude, the words and diction scant
Of wit and force, the style inelegant.
Yet much there can a careful reader find
Like to repay a wise, reflecting mind.
Let him forget the verses' outward sound,
And keep the inward sense with them upbound.
Who doubts that truth from trifles can be drawn,
Or that from stories wisdom oft is born?
Great mysteries oft in simple tales lie hid,
And precious truth is cheaply garmented.
Whate'er of moral worth a book affords,
Keep it, to teach its lesson by its words.
I marvel, pondering on antiquity,
How well we do to note it, you and I;
How present times from past are altered quite;
First becomes last, and day grows into night.
So light serene is into darkness brought,
Fool passes into sage, sage into—nought.
Cato grows dull in wit, no longer ready
Ulysses' tongue, the shifting breeze grows steady;
Who late was dumb, Ulysses doth surpass,
And Cato yields to him who witless was.
He who in stress of war was wise and sage
Is proved a dotard in a peaceful age.
He who in war-time showed but little sense

1

In peace-time gains a Cato's sapience.
And infants (what more marvellous still appears)
Though scarce yet born steal the sage Nestor's years;
A beardless boy is fancied to outreach
Cato in wisdom, Cicero in speech;
All that beneath the lunar sphere doth lie
He can unlock and probe its mystery.
Whate'er the character a man should show,
Whate'er the skill, your wish will make him so;
If such the time, the place, the company,
If such the critic, just so will he be.
So seems a wall when whitened pure and clean,
Behind would nought but mud and filth be seen.
So paint clothes dirt, so jewels beautify,
And rotting boards 'neath golden plating lie.
Who in himself no power hath to stand
Or rise, must seek aid from another's hand.
But how ridiculous, if helped to rise
He struts vainglorious in the people's eyes!
Though it should from his own achievement flow,
Pride's still a fault, but less by far, I trow.
An ass, though he may hold a monarchy
And rule the folk, an ass will ever be.
An ass in lion's place would harsher prove
Than lion's self, and more resentment move.
An ass draped in a lion's skin is known
By undue pride and vanity o'erflown.
A thing pretended need not rouse offence
If moderation governs the pretence.
But angry pride impatient in new seat
Leaps ever headlong to its own defeat.
Now to himself he must once more return.
Poor ass, he's learnt his fortune to unlearn.
His lion's semblance failed, and with it went
All that he dreamed of rich emolument.

2

Whatever through his folly he has lost,
Was not his own, he'll never feel the cost.
What was his own before, conferred by none,
Remains to him, so nought of that is gone.
Who cannot be a lion, or sustain
The lion's burden, ass let him remain.
Far better therefore had he left alone
Another's goods than hazarded his own,
And ridicule therewith and base dishonour known.

THE ADVENTURES OF BURNEL THE ASS

There was an Ass with ears of monstrous size,
Who wished with them his tail to equalise.
It was too short—though not for use, he said;
He grieved because it did not match his head.
So, lest it suffer more abbreviation,
He called the doctors in for consultation;
For they, he thought, might all their art apply,
And so make good Nature's deficiency.
But Galen said: "Two feet of tail suffice
For any donkey; just take my advice,
Don't try for more; the more you lengthen it,
Letting it trail along the muddy street,
The filthier it will be. So be content,
Or else you may well find, whereas you meant
To make it long you'll only make it short.
Value what Nature sends, nor hold as nought
What she has given. Believe me, that old tail
Stuck on your rump is of far more avail
Than one that's new. But no, it doesn't please,
You want a better. All our surgeries

Will only make a worse one. Any moke
Can have his tail cut off; but it's no joke
To make a new one grow. Life's short, Art's long,
No time to lose when things are going wrong.
Treatment oft fails and cures are hard to work;
Dangers remain for sure, and causes lurk
Concealed; the laws of medicine differ far
From what both you and others think they are.
Not even high skill can always sickness heal,
Medicine is set in balance, tips the scale
In equal measure both to good and ill,
Heals one but not another. Though the will
Be there, the power oft lacks, the doctor fails
To give the longed-for help to him who ails.
God's Grace performs, he doth but minister.
The precepts of our art, then, we who hear
Must practise faithfully; yet even so
We cannot what you wish on you bestow.
'Tis God alone that heals; the will is ours,
But His the power; they whom His aid empowers
Can heal, our aid He needs not; we make use
Of varied kinds of pigment, herb and juice;
His word alone makes whole; healers are we
In name, but God in true reality.
Remember then, that tail He gave retain,
You foolish ass, nor further things in vain
Seek after, and to what you have hold on,
Lest what you have you haply find is gone.
Stay as your doctor left you, I entreat,
Till He return himself and change your state.
Safer a humble state with happy mind
Than high position with distress combined.
Foolish ambition fosters many dreams
Which give not help but hindrance to its schemes.
Why, your own ears your nature do confess,

4

And show the folly of your purposes.
Why, your two ears could three such bodies cover,
And still there would be stuff remaining over.
Such portents to all eyes themselves display,
The less you have the better, I should say.
'Long-ears' you're called: the facts confirm the joke,
And you're the laughing-stock of all the folk.
Two portents in one body! even more
Will people point and hold their sides and roar.
What if your tail to five-foot length should grow?
By head and tail they'd pull you to and fro.
Great things become great folk; you're small, then why
Should longer tail more usefulness imply?
'Tis safer then, I say, to keep that tail
Than graft a new one, which may not avail;
For even a tail engrafted might not strike
(And if it did I've never heard the like!)
Saying is easy, monstrous hard the deed;

Words quickly flow, but time spins out the doing.
Saying is light, for wind and air give speed;
Action is weighty, and retards the going.
Speech is for all, but speech must grow to act,
Else it is wind, pure wind that mocks the view;
Speech is for all, but to wed speech in fact
With deed—think only—few attain thereto.
Both are from Him, who all created things
Sustains and moves, Who knows their every case;
Who makes, remakes, all into being brings
And governs, constant in all time and space.
What, of what sort, He made you, you will be,
Obstinate one, ay, even though you resist;
For under Him is all mortality;
He and none other caused you to exist.
Accept (you must) whatever from your birth
He has decreed for you up to this day;
What you supposed might be is nothing worth;
None can do aught when Nature says him nay.
Why, foolish ass, the nobler, larger beasts
For longer tails make no such vain requests.
Theirs are the shorter, yet hind, goat and bear
Make no petition, nor the hunted hare,
Nor yet the hart that leaps on the high hill;
Why then should you the air with plainings fill—
Are you a nobler, holier thing than they?
Your head is large, your body's grand; so, pray,
Set these against your tail's deficiency,
And feel no shame at inequality.
In length of tail King Louis of the French
Does not surpass you, no, nor all his bench
Of bishops either. So then my advice
Is to hold firmly on, nor sacrifice
That which you have; because your present state
Might, if you do so, soon deteriorate.

GALEN'S STORY OF THE TWO COWS

Now hear a story. When I was a lad
Upon my father's farm, two cows we had
Among the rest, Bicornis light of hue,
Brunetta dark. One winter's eve these two
Leaving their well-known pasture ground (the way
Through muddy tracks and miry marshland lay)
Cut off by gathering darkness from their byre
Lay down, as cows will, in the mud and mire.
Night came and sudden frost, which far and wide
All that before was soft solidified.
Mud hardens into stone; spring, pond and lake
Grow marble; channels hold with tightened grip
The waves they cherished, nor allow to slip
In wonted course away. The waters make
So many bridges: passage smooth and free
Before denied is granted readily.
Their miry tails, held fast by miry ground,
Hold fast the cows, in strict coercion bound.
Soon with returning morn they too would fain
Return, but effort mocks their hopes, in vain
They struggle hard; ice glues them to the soil.
Worn out, they stay their striving, yet the toil
Renew, in silent pain or loud complaint.
All's vain: the force opposing without cease
By its own natural strength forbids release.
But now Bicornis hears the lowings faint
Of her small calf, whom newly born at home
She'd left in stall, lest following it should come
To find her. Toiling then with all her might,

7

Yet fruitlessly, at last in desperate plight
'One hope' she cries, 'remains, our tails to sever,
Which chain us here, poor cows, how hard soever
We try, and take all hope of home away.
What profit or what glory can I say
My tail has brought me; in it there's no guerdon,
Could I return 'twould ever be a burden.
Down to the ground it hangs and gathers mire,
And now, stuck fast, it keeps me from the byre.
Better by far the substance ne'er to cherish
By whose effect I here am like to perish.
The law provides—or so the lawyers tell—
The cause removed, the thing caused goes as well.
Part's better lost than whole, and tail than head,
One small by many good things is outweighed.
I'd rather tail with leg were torn away
Than that my life should cease this very day.
Perchance again I'll tarry in this place,
And once more be imprison'd in like case,
If now my tail be severed, surely more
Secure will my return be than before.
If I should die so will my daughter too,
Not five days old; for her sake must I do

This thing, though for my sake I did it not.
This tail's the part that oft has wounding got
By teeth of dogs; near half is torn away
Already: how much left, alas! today.
What they have spared, to her I sacrifice,
Both duty this and profit in my eyes.
Why then delay what I'm resolved upon?
An urgent case needs action quickly done.'
She spoke, and knife in hand cut off her tail,
Then started homeward; yet first made avail
The knife, ere going, to Brunetta's use,
Her body from detainment thus to loose.
But she, less headstrong or more prudent made,

9

Heard out her sister, but refused the blade.
She answered: 'Why this trouble, foolish one?
God grant I should not take your counsel! None
Should act with rashness in adversity,
But use restraint. When fortune falters, try
(So I've been told) to hold the curb-rein tight.
For impulse gathering strength does nothing right.
When things go wrong, seek not wrong-headed force,
But honest help and counsel; such a course
Wise Cato urges, for rough deeds may mar
What's soft and gentle, therefore better far
Be not impatient; time itself may heal
When reason fails; the burden that we feel
So heavy, changes may alleviate.
Time passes, masters, servants change their state.
None can foresee or shun what fate may show;
Fear nought before it happens, better so
Than worry, sure of ill; distress has taught
While oft success has hindered or has brought
A pleasure to be feared; more rarely leads
Experience of grief to faulty deeds.
While yet the foes lay sundered in the field
Troy stood, nor yet did her defences yield.
Peace overthrew her walls, not battle stress,
Not royal arms but her own slothfulness.
Scarce comes good fortune, rare and weak its course;
Ill fortune coming strikes with whirlwind force.
Fortune to me has long been kind, then why
Disdain to bear some slight adversity?
For my duress will not endure a year;

10

Not one day yet has passed while this I bear.
Far rougher substance should I have, I trow,
Than mud for fetters, were I thrust below
Deep in the dungeon of a prince or king;
Of iron then would be my fettering.
And iron fetters even kings may bind,
So mine a lighter fate than theirs I find.
Five years long their imprisonment, may be,
Endures, perhaps three days will set me free;
Light Zephyrs will renew the South wind's reign,
And all the meads be soft with mud again.
Then without cost my bonds will melt away,
And my tail still remain. This very day
I could have severed it, but penitent
Had I been ever then and ill-content.
One night secured the captive, and perchance
One night will bring her quick deliverance.
Whom winter harms let summer's grace relieve,
To one man's lot another's comfort give.
So different changes their own seasons bring,
Now one and now another honouring.
Let one man's losses and diminished state
Another's richer store recuperate.
For none's so high, so far above the rest,
That need of other's help he's ne'er confest.
Various the differences of time and change,
And compacts too from strength to weakness range.
So we have seen a hurrying wain o'erset
By a small bush that in its course it met,
A small device lay mighty towers low,
And a light touch high battlements o'erthrow.
Light raindrops can fierce hurricanes assuage,
And the North-easter calm the ocean's rage,
A tiny cause great perils turn aside,
By a small stick mad dogs are terrified,

A little water makes the mounting flames subside.
So though my tail's my last extremity,
Nought have I that's of more utility.
It's heavy and not comely, yet, I guess,
Summer redeems its disadvantages.
More safety than two horns my single tail
Affords in time of summer; like a flail
It deals its blows against my enemies,
Fans wasps away, disperses gnats and flies.
Of shield and sword and axe it plays the part,
Of bow and arrow, firebrand, sling and dart.
My body's faithful nurse, it tends my hide,
And wipes off dust adhering to my side.
It wipes, it laves, one for all labouring,
Last of my limbs, yet first in ministering.
Consider to what honour or what use
Their owner's other single limbs conduce:
More than they all, yea even than my head
Does it bestow; by it are covered
The marks of our weak sex, concealed thereby
From public gaze; thus in variety
Of season doth it varied service show,
Welcome to me, and doubly welcome now.
For now I fear the times I needs must fear
(Nor fears in vain who well-known ills doth fear).
For when I contemplate my suffering
Past and to come, I say: Soon comes the spring;
Soon will the gnats revive, as yet kept under
By frost and ice; soon summer's violent heat
Will scorch the land and split the herd asunder
And send them scattering on frightened feet.
The gnat, that deadly, that most poisonous pest,
Of all the plagues on earth the deadliest,
O'er every field will drive in frenzied spate
Us wretched cows: no more our usual gait,

But, stung and bitten, we shall leap and rear,
Kick up our heels and seem to sail on air.
Trust me, that day's not far on which the cow
Will need that tail she so despises now.
That day will show how tails salvation bring
(Summer forewarns by winter's presaging).
That day will make old cows and oxen too
And heifers mind what tails are meant to do.
That day her tail will poor Bicornis mind
And ere lose head before than tail behind.
That day will raise our tails to value high,
Cheaper today than broken crockery.
That day like Judgment Day will everywhere

Be full of awe and trembling and of fear.
That day will count our tails and look them over,
And which are good and which are bad discover.
That day between them will discriminate,
Which are in clean and which in muddy state.
That is the day (ask any heifer) when
If she were given two tails she'd wish for ten.
That is the day when speeding on apace
The gadfly comes, chief torment of our race.
That is the day which sharp-toothed gnats will send
Upon the herd, to harry without end.
That is the day whose coming all should fear
Before it comes. What joy could one live clear
Of that dread day! at thought of it I quail,
I fear it worse than death, when save my tail
Nothing can give me safety. None can shun
Or swarming gnats or scorching heat of sun
By hiding; nor do flies and scorching glare
Harm beasts alone, so too do herdsmen fare.
Yet none to other, herdsmen to his horde,
Nor bull to heifer succour can afford.
For help or harm that day there can avail
Nothing of other, only my own tail.
Its safety is my safety, nought's secure

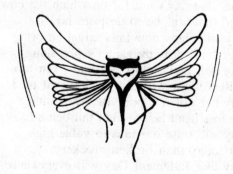

Save where no gnat can go. So I am sure
That though thereby I'm held in dire constraint
My spirit will not from distress grow faint.
Five days I'll yet endure. The frost will go
Perchance by then. I'd rather suffer so
Than let long months of summer's fiery breath
And bites of gadflies torture me to death?
Even while she speaks the season changes,
Refreshed by its brief winter drowse
The earth revives; the sun now ranges
Higher in heaven with searching rays;
The frost dissolves, the water flows
Again, each wood and field displays
Its former scene; from prison free
Nature enjoys her liberty.
Brunetta rises up, her tail thus freed,
And starts in haste for home along the mead.
Bicornis spied her sister as she went,
And beat her breast, and uttered sad lament:

LAMENT OF BICORNIS

"Alas, what have I done? why madly did I strive
    My own defeat to hasten so?
Ah me, from headlong acts what cruel ends derive!
    Impatience—how it leads to woe!
Ah me, ah wretched me! how pitiable am I!
    For whom remains nought but ah me!
Ah me! that I to all who live both far and nigh
    A laughing-stock must ever be.
Alas, why with my tail did Fate my life not slit,
    That head and tail might meet at last?

Why could not river draw me in or earthy pit,
    Or far-flung brand of lightning blast?
Headlong I was—then why not follow my own beck
    And headlong fall from mountain top?
Alas! why did not halter tighten round my neck,
    And breath and guilt together stop?

Why did not deadly plague that wanders here and there
    Or sudden death my poor life take,
Quick death that solves all doubts, sole medicine for care?
    Which soon an end to mine will make.
For winter now is past, spring days new strength receive,
    And summer's advent terrifies.
Bicornis doomed to die will as a warning live,
    And by her folly fools make wise.
Let headstrong haste be warned, that hurrying heeds no fence,
    From hastening to its own defeat.
Let pleasure satisfied, through sage experience,
    With little, nought as little treat,
Nor aught that chance may lose. But why do I complain?
    Let those to come two precepts know:
That's nought and less than nought (so long it doth remain)
    What we possess; but should it go,
That which was nought ranks high. Esteem, though small it be
    Whate'er you fear to lose, as gold.
So I my tail, possessed, did scorn—now gone from me
    Of wealth beyond all else I hold."

        But now is come lush summer time,
        Painting the land with all the prime
        Of flowers, the woods are gay with leaves,
        Colour of blossoms interweaves
        The grassy meadows. Birds appear,
        Their prison broken, sweet to hear
        In tribute to the country round.
        The nightingale, by silence bound

16

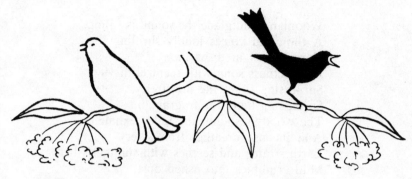

Through wintry months, time lost redeems,
And fills with music all the grove.
The lark that heralds the first beams
Of dawning day, the turtle-dove
And warbling blackbird duly follow,
And, to his season true, the swallow.
The cuckoo greets the springtime too,
New times but old refrain, nought new.

Woodland and glade the sound is filling,
A thousand voices loudly shrilling
Harmonious in disharmony;
In sweetness song with scent doth vie;
Surpassing flutes the minstrelsy,
Surpassing balm the fragrancy;
The woods resound, the fields exhale,
And incense breathes from every pale.
Earth strains and seethes with summer's lust;
Mud crumbles into ashen dust,
Corpses breed worms, the ground breeds flies,
Gnats vex the air in companies;
Plague of the farmland, gadflies fierce
With bites that rend and stings that pierce
Disrupt the herd; by terror riven
They go, o'er hills, through byways driven.
Sweating and burning hot they tear
Through wood and glade in wild stampede,
Herd mixed with herdsmen; far they spread
Scattering pell-mell; among the rest
Brunetta (with Bicornis near
Gallantly in her peril striving)
Resists the flies and wasps, that pest
Immoderate, sweeping, lashing, giving
More than she takes. At least a swarm,
Relentless, multitudinous, hounding
Bicornis undefended, where
She flees pursue her, wheresoe'er
She turns attack her, stinging, wounding.
What can she do, to deadly harm
Exposed? distracted still she ran
While yet she could. (But never can
A running foot outstrip a wing
Of flier, flight o'erpasses foot.
Arms obtain peace by victory, but

He quickly falls who none can bring
To combat.) Still with failing strength
She fled the gadflies thronging all
Around her (shame doth no less gall
Than wounding), till foredone at length
She fails, and falls on hilly ground;
But at the last when, near to death
She saw her sorrowing friends around,
Gaining a little strength and breath
Once more, she lifted up her head,
And these last words of farewell said:
'How grievous is this day, how memorable,
To all that live my mournful fate can tell.
Yet death's not hard; could I yet more life see,
Harder to bear than death would living be.
Nought sweeter to the wretched than to die!
Death brings me glad relief from misery.
My life a pattern gave, my death shall give
To all a warning that for aye shall live.
Learn then how close to ruin pride doth dwell
That knows not reason; aught that prospers well
May impulse overthrow; unstable that
Which impulse stablishes. Learn too to rate
As nothing what ephemeral pleasure brings
And falsely claims its own. All worldly things
Has Nature given in common use to keep,
Nought in propriety of ownership.
Learn then the unhappy story of my tail,
And how it caused my death." Nought could avail
Her further effort, all her strength was past.
"Bruny, farewell," she sighed, and breathed her last.
The herdsmen therefore lest her name should die
Inscribed these words on her tomb's masonry:

> "She by her folly taught the wise;
> Now dead a prey to worms she lies."

All this I saw myself and now have told,
Burnel, for your instruction. What you hold
Let that suffice, for if the truth be said,
Saving your honour, you're a muttonhead,
And your scheme's folly. Best go home. You can't
Find any drugs to do the thing you want.
Though every leech you in the world could find
Swore he could graft a tail on your behind,
'Twould be but words—though I will not deny
A tail might grow if treated properly.
Broken or bruised—can be made whole again;
But severed—so for ever must remain.

What's cut but not cut off can treatment bear,
But dead with living never can cohere.
Let tail with body in due compact be,
Tail then might grow in length considerably.
But mind—the cost we have to calculate;
The drugs are numerous and the outlay great.
Difficult cures must swollen purses bleed,
And deep-set wounds of deep-laid wealth have need.
Would it not be enough to make addition
Of a whole ell, to meet your high ambition?"
He murmured his assent with smiling face;
The noise re-echoed through the market-place.
Galen went on: "Off to Salerno then,
And with all speed be out and back again.
Buy there whate'er you need; see you don't waste
Time on the road; with all four feet make haste,
Add a fifth if you can! Just pay the cost:
I'll see you find none of my labour's lost.
You pay the money, I'll apply the skill,
If their old power my hands remember still.
Quick then and get your passport, that will lend
Speed to your journey. You have many a friend,
Some dear ones, who will money gifts supply.
Easy perhaps to find the cures; yet I
Fear they may not be found so easily.
But take for them, to bring them home again,
Vessels in plenty. Spare no toil or pain
In packing, lest they perish on the way,
And seal them too, lest aught should go astray.
And now (you've skill to write) on parchment clear
Write down the cures which you'll have need of here.
Some marble-fat, fresh milk of kite or goose,
Some fear of wolf, some speed of running luce,
Cool shade of furnace heated seven times hot,
A foal that on a she-mule has been got,

21

A seven years' treaty between hare and hound;
Of peacock's scream (tail not yet grown)—a pound;
Some warpless cloth unwoven, red of hue,
Some ass's laughter (found of course by you),
Some saffron milt of herring or of bee,
Some kisses which the lark has lovingly
Sent to her falcon, liver of cheese-mite
Or foot or blood; of blessed Christmas night,
Which for your use full long enough should prove,
A little portion; from the Mount of Jove
Three pounds and fifteen ounces you should bring;
And while among the Alps you're travelling
During the night of John the Baptist take
A little snow that's fallen; tail of snake
And scarlet viper—very useful they,
But not a penny for them should you pay.
Collect all these (they must be new), then pack
Them carefully and hoist them on your back."
So Galen spoke; and the ass stooping low
His suppliant head down to the ground did bow,
And made reply: "All this with willing heart
Will I perform. I'll make a speedy start
And speedily return. It's my affair,
None other's; so be sure I'll do whate'er
You bid me. Lazy was I wont to be,
But I'll be quick now if God prospers me.
I'm going straightway; bless me as I go,
That life and road good fortune may bestow."
Then Galen smiling and in foreign phrase
Gives blessing: "The Almighty," so he prays
"Send you a thousand curses, and your tail
Win you ten thousand more! May rain and hail
And snow and sleet companionship afford!
Water and thistles be your drink and board,
And dews your shelter! Wheresoe'er you turn

22

May odious dogs be barking at your stern!"
"Amen!" said Burnel, and with warm embrace
Saluted Galen; all the market-place
Amen, Amen repeated, and around
The city's streets re-echoed with the sound.
Hurrying away he stumbled at the gate;
Some laughed, and neighbours said: 'Unfortunate!
This shows you'd best turn back." But no, thought he,
Bad start, but better fortune presently.
The way is long; it won't be always so.
I've been well schooled in hardship, and well know
How to endure it. From my mother's womb
Life has been hard for me; there's been no room
For dainty courses or for drunkenness.
Thistles and burs provide the tastiest mess,
And rain's my drink; that is the healthiest way;
Plain living and high thinking, so they say.
I'm slow and lazy, but I'd lazier be
If I were used to dine luxuriously.
Nay, even your rich man is no better for't
If he puts down too much champagne and port.
Wine's not for me—makes wise men lose their wit,
And does a mort of harm: I'll none of it!
My parents carried it, as all could see,
Outside, not inside; no, it's not for me.
So then I'll mill it, but not swill it, ever,
Lest I fall victim to quotidian fever,
Or catch a quartan or a scurvy too,
If I drank wine, as my folk never do.
Four reasons then urge me to abstinence
(Although the stuff does titillate the sense),
To save my pocket, keep disease away,
And save my mind and body from decay.
Who can but doesn't shun a threatening evil,
Can take his sorrows with him to the devil!"

After twelve days of long peregrination
He sees the high walls of his destination.
There with knees bent and arms outstretched he pays
His suppliant vows to Heaven, and thus he prays:
"By blessed Julian's merits may the Lord
Show us his favour, and grant bed and board!
Keep harm away, plank bridges, panniers double,
Which in my own land cause me plenty trouble
May never countryman or sack be found
Here, no, nor any mill where corn is ground
May goads be blunt, the dogs be deaf and dumb,
And to my ears no hateful barking come
May I, when some kind farmer puts me up,
Off rainwater and nice rough thistles sup
May all those goods I want be cheap as trash,
Buyers be few and salesmen short of cash
May wares be numerous, money value good,
The weather rainy and the roads all mud
May Heaven prosperity and blessing send,
That sooner may my errand have an end."
He finished, and soon after reached the town,
Entered an inn and laid his tired limbs down.
Rising next morn he seeks the goods to buy,
But baffled goes in sad perplexity.
Four days about the city streets he fares,
In fruitless search for non-existent wares.
A London merchant spied him as he strayed,
Took note of him and thus accosting said:
"You are a Deputy of note, I see;

Important are those wares in high degree
For which you seek. Whoever sent you here
Was wise and wealthy also, that is clear.
Your face and figure plainly indicate
Both who you are and whence you've come—a great
Person indeed; though foreign garb you wear,
In your own land you'll be no foreigner.
All your great house, how they must feel concern,
What vows and prayers uplift for your return!
England's my birthplace, London is my home;
On bishop's business lately did I come.
Nature had set his nose a-tilt, and he
Required that Art should find a remedy.
So on account of this unhappy—bent,
Four of us to these foreign parts were sent.
One year passed, then another: now bereft
Of my three friends by one fell stroke I'm left.
Look, I have wares, which would effect, I'm sure
Could you but take them home, a wondrous cure.
All that you came to look for here abroad
I've got it in my house all sealed and stored.
I can't get home; I've fallen into debt;
The expenses were too great, and here I'm set!
But how I miss the land I hold so dear
All the more keenly that I'm stranded here.
News has just come, my father's passed away;
And so has my old master, so they say.
Now look, I've ten glass jars, filled to the top
With all your paper mentions, in my shop.
Just give me what I paid myself, and then
Tomorrow, well-equipped, start home again.
Beyond that sum I would not ask a bean—
We're strangers here together—I'm not so mean.
Yet this I ask: you have a saintly air,
So don't forget me when you say a prayer."

Then straightway Burnel counted out the cash,
And took for it ten vessels full of trash;
And then the contract thus to stabilise
He asked the merchant's name: he thus replies:
"Trickman I'm called, my father just the same;
I'm London born; Jill is my mother's name;
Julie's my sister, known in many lands,
Trickie's my wife, joined in true wedlock's bands.
Now you tell me what noble name you own,
That I may not forget you when you're gone."
"Burnel they call me" said the ass, "and I
Enjoy in all lands notoriety
In name and person. Princes of the land

And even kings I serve when they command,
Though I'm no servant born. My father too
And grandsire owned the same obedience due;
So I by right paternal did succeed,
And of my service all the Court have need.
Should the king meet me as he goes abroad
He gives place, ay, he steps from off the road,
And I go on my way. Yet one offence
Torments me, one sore, plaguy pestilence,
The rustic with his goad and knotted whips,
And pack of dogs up-leaping round his hips;
My father, all my race he did detest,
Ay, all that ever were. But I like best
The ways of prince and noble, pleasant folk,
Who meet you with a laugh, a word, a joke,
And often on their arm a comely lass.
Bless you, says king, when in the road I pass;
Curse you, says rustic. Nasty, villainous wretch,
May fever torture him and scabrous itch!
May his head ache, may gout torment his jaw,
From sole of foot to crown may he be sore
With ulcers, foul with worms and putrefaction,
His belly flow with constant liquefaction
Both night and day, so he can never ride
Or go afoot; may a hard master chide
And rule him ever, quarrelling and strife
Perpetual reign between him and his wife!
Him I commend to Satan, from whose dung
All rustics (like enough) they say are sprung!
Ay, if I could I'd wipe them from earth's face,
That neither town nor country find them place."
So saying Burnel with exultant mind
Prepares to leave Italian land behind.
Morn comes, he pays his thankful vows to God,
Then passes from the city with his load.

When fortune smiles how hard it is to see
The easy fall, the near fatality.
Now on the road to Lyons city bent
He took a path that through a cornfield went,
Thinking no harm; but by ill chance was spied
By one of the White Brothers (close beside
Was their domain), who sent with angry shout
Four huge, fierce hounds against him, calling out:
"You'll take a short cut through our cornfield,
    will you?
The highway was too narrow? Wait until you
Learn the right road from these four mastiffs here;
You won't make that mistake again, I swear.
By my top-boots, you'll find you'd best have stayed
On the high road, for all its turns, not made
This short cut; ay, you'll find it not so short
When these have done their business, as you thought!"
The dogs thus urged assailed him one by one,
On this side and on that, and made him run.
In turn they catch him up, each savage hound,
And bite and pull and force him to the ground.
But Grimbald first with cruel snapping jaw
Had left his tail half what it was before.
He, quite forgetting what his burden was,
And that his precious vessels were of glass,
When the dog leapt and bit him, down he fell
Upon the ground and all his wares as well.
All the jars perished in that single crash:
A simple cause a fragile thing can smash.

With hard toil won but lightly made as nought
Unending grief they to their owner brought.
There was but left what one could nothing call,
Fragments of glass were left, and that was all.
Into thin air the substance all had passed,
His hopes were fled, his labour gone to waste.
Now for his tail he grieves and Grimbald's bite,
Now that the money spent has vanished quite.
Each blow brings anguish; one enough would be:
A double loss brings double misery.
Scarce could he reckon which torments him most,
The tail, the money or the labour, lost.
The toil is spent, the gold he'll see no more;
While a whole tail can no-one now restore.
Anguish and grief and shame afflict his mind;
His anguish grows through grief and shame combined.
A prey to dogs poor Burnel rolls in pain;
Scarce doth his life (nought else) to him remain.
Then brother Fromund—savage beast indeed
Was Fromund, just like all his wicked breed,
And false dissembler also—moving slow
Towards Burnel at last begins to go.
Slow mover he, save when at the bell's peal
His fat paunch leads the way to evening meal.
With tread spondaic, slow as any ass's,
He comes, as when to Lauds at night he passes.
"Ho! there," he cried, and called the dogs away.
And gave with outstretched hand a Benedicité.
"No benediction for you," Burnel cried,
"But malediction on your head abide
For ever! Did you learn from Benedict
With mastiffs fierce poor travellers to afflict?
Did Benedict so teach you? Can this be
A new command on high authority,
A new-found rule for your observance passed

29

At Cîteaux, when within this twelve-month last
The fathers met and made this ordinance?
Is this a rule that orders you, perchance,
To harry the Pope's Legate with your hounds,
To deal without due reason death and wounds
To such a man? Hither have I been sent,
Bearing to our Lord Pontiff medicament
Of highest value. Stranger, traveller here
I took a path that was both broad and clear,
Well-trodden, though it through a cornfield led;
There was no thought of mischief in my head.
I deemed it was a highway; what I did
Was error, not intention, God forbid.
Light punishment to petty crimes is due;
Grant it a fault what I have done, grant too
It should be punished, yet the punishment
Was too severe; it must be ever bent
To fit the crime's degree; if too severe,
It is itself a crime. While journeying here
As Nuncio of the Pope, I took a road,
A by-road as it chanced; sure there was owed
Some fear and reverence to the Pope whereby
Should be excused an erring emissary.
You magnified the fault: who in this land
Doth fear the Lord and heed the Pope's command?
This wrong to God and not to me is done:
Let the Pope be my champion, God his own.
Your sin upon the Pontiff will redound,
And all the Curia suffer from the wound.
So dire a crime, so horrible a deed,
Excess so grave must surely vengeance breed.
If Rome use not the utmost of her strength
With the Lord Pope so slighted, sure at length
None will to any Power due reverence show,
But what each pleases he'll be free to do.

The loss and disgrace the Pope sustains,
I bear in my own wounding what remains.
The damage at two thousand marks I rate.
Without the toil or outlay's estimate.
But how to rate dishonour? He will know,
Who bears the slight, who bears the honour too.
Upon the Pope both hurt and loss redound,
Each has its weight, wide open lies each wound.
A weighty fault he'll soon with ease remit:
A light one will with weightier pains be quit.
Hurt honour tears and prayers can expiate;
Lest that he seem o'ermuch to vindicate;
But money loss for mercy ne'er can plead,
A bargain there would prove him mild indeed.
If the Cistercians can refund the cost,
Then all will be made good of what he's lost.
They must pay tithes, and (what they cannot bear)
Breeches on their behinds for ever wear.
They'll be confined to cloisters, forfeit all
Their precious pasture-lands, or face a call
For full three thousand marks, with interest;
If they're not quick, the fine will be increased
To a full million. But what of my case?
What vengeance is for me? What can replace
These sores and lacerations? True, the Pope
Will make decree that no White Brother hope
To leave his cloister but he must submit
To these three penalties, transgressing it:
No wine at table, no cooked greens to see,
And this hard rule perpetual to be.
So will the Pope by Canon law my cause
Right willingly avenge, but Civil Laws
Must champion me as well and all my own;
This will I have throughout the world laid down,
If e'er I live to see it: whoever spies

31

These Converts (nay, from their activities
Perverts were best) outside the Abbey wall
Shall of right eye and foot relieve them all,
And, save a bell be hanging round their necks,
Of member too and what's belonging. Breeks
I'll bid them wear, wine must they never taste,
Fish, flesh and eggs be from their meals displaced;
For all let two cooked greens suffice, I say,
Nay, uncooked rather, save on festal day.
These sanctions all my folk shall render sure,
That to eternity they may endure.
The Pontiff too shall give them confirmation,
And all the Court subscribe their attestation."

BROTHER FROMUND'S ATTEMPTED DECEIT

Fromund heard this and quaked, and terrified
Beyond belief, "If the Abbot hear," he cried,
"And sure he will, so grave will this appear,
Then death is certain for me, yes, I fear
The deadly sack. What stark insanity
To vex with dogs the Papal emissary!
I never thought 'twas he—how could I know?
What madness drove me on to treat him so?
But now I've need to act, and quickly too,
I've need of help and counsel, for it's true
That if this fellow gets away alive
The business can't be hidden. I must contrive
With flatteries to keep him hereabout
Until the time when I can knock him out!
Else for our Order is destruction come,
And all our houses too. I must be mum,

32

And act with cunning, get him far away
From all the folk. There'd be the deuce to pay
If anything leaked through about this matter;
Things would be far, far worse with people's chatter.
Not only that I fear: the Brothers too,
They frighten me; ay, if the Brothers knew!
For people's talk to some extent allows
Controlling, but it's worse than forty rows
When they get mad. You'd be in the same case
Telling a secret in the market-place
As here among the bretheren; it's one town,
But they're a thousand. What you don't want known
Don't breathe to anyone. Trustworthiness?
That's not worth trusting; trust has many a face,
Changes with seasons. Who trusts more than one
Is not safe to be trusted. I alone
Am going to know of this; I'm going to do it
Where no-one else can hear or see or know it.
Why then waste time? I'll go in all humility
And pardon beg, and say with much civility
I'll make good all his losses. I'll deceive
The stupid idiot, cause him to believe
I'm a true friend. He's easy to outwit;
I'd tell him what I like, he'll swallow it."
Then went he humbly and for pardon prayed:
More than Burnel had lost would be repaid:
He offered lodging, hospitable fare,
Soft bed for weary limbs, salubrious air,
Physician's aid, convivial feasting, too,
All that he dreamed of, all he wished to do
He there would find; let him but come, he said,
And see the place himself: there was a glade
Near Lyons by the waters of the Rhone,
Embowered in trees, where all that for its own
The human heart desires the earth supplies,

33

A blessed spot, a second Paradise;
The master of the land himself will see
The house provided, all agreeably
To his own pleasure, none will say him nay;
A servant of his own he'll have, to pay
Due heed and come when bidden; all he'll find
Willing to serve and please; he need but mind
The manner of their service to dictate
To these or those: all will upon him wait.
Nor will he be as a newcomer there,
A stranger who will on the morrow fare
Homeward, nay, as a freeman will he be,
A citizen in perpetuity.
With voice and hand he plies his exhortations,
His promises and prayers and adjurations
Burnel to this assented willingly,
Yet made condition that the dogs must die.
And thus dissembling (for he knew the guile
Of Fromund) veiled his features in a smile,
Then to himself he spoke two words, yet so
That Fromund should not hear them whispered low.
"Different the donkey's and the driver's thought,
And different hopes to different ends are brought.
Virtue sometimes can wickedness outpace,
A clever cure forestall a serious case.
Fraud is o'ercome by fraud and art by art,
Cunning gives way to cunning's quicker start."
So Fromund seized a cudgel, and in wrath
Dispatched the dogs, then hastened on his path.
Now while on the high bank of Rhone these two
Burnel ahead and Fromund next did go,
The ass, perceiving how the margin steep
Was fit for sudden death and deadly leap,
With sudden thrust hurled Fromund from the bank
Into the stream; he to the bottom sank.

Trapped by the waves he therein perishes,
A victim of his own deceitfulness.
Then Burnel raised his voice in exultation,
And shouted forth resounding jubilation:

BURNEL'S SONG OF TRIUMPH

Sing out, brother asses, high festival hold!
Open throats in thanksgiving and song!
Sing joyfully, asses, bray out loud and bold,
With kettle-drum, rattle and gong!
For Grimbald has perished, his comrades as well,
One death has seized enemies four;
And Fromund is drowned, in the river he fell;
He is mocked by his own wicked lore.
Brother Fromund has fallen and perished, oh joy!
'Twas he set the treacherous gin;
The clever man plotted the fool to destroy,
But the fool pushed the clever man in.
'Twas he digged the pit, and in it was he caught;
One jump, and the journey was done;
Steep cliff, rushing river, deep channel—untaught
I taught him his jumping, alone.
Let the river exult o'er the glorious deed,
For Fromund is fallen, sing praise!
Let earth with her blossoms and flowers give heed,
And melodious psalmody raise!

So Fromund died; his body from the wave
Extracted to his native earth they gave.
Which Burnel passing saw with flowing tear,
And caused his tomb this epitaph to bear:
For Fromund dead his foe who's living yet
These lasting lines upon his tomb doth set.

Clever and quick was he, and thought to cheat
The slow and stupid, but himself was beat
At his own game, and so was foolish shown
By the quick leap which drowned him in the Rhone.
So cunning outdoes cunning, fraud gives way
To fraud, and each due retribution pay.
Brethren, from wicked Fromund's leap be wise
Such roguery as his to recognise.

BURNEL DECIDES TO GO TO PARIS

After this last adventure grim
Eager in heart, in every limb,
Burnel's in haste to hurry home.
But since to nought his funds have come
He needs must beg, and as he goes
In progress slow his memory flows
O'er what befell, what at the first
Galen advised; the more immersed
He is in such consideration
The keener his self-accusation.
"No sage am I Burnel," he said,
"But lazy and a muttonhead,
Dull-witted, slow to move, an ass
In primis—so I ever was,
So born, so till my life expire
Shall I remain. Stupid my sire,
My mother too, most stupid she,
Our Nature's gift, stupidity.
What Nature gave, what from the prime
Has stayed, will stay, and through long time
Remains for ever. If I think

36

Who, what am I, in thought I sink
To mean estate, to nothingness.
Lo, strength and vigour, time and stress
Have I now wasted; soon old age
Is near, nought written on the page
Of life (the facts will verify
My words) save crass stupidity.
Age and dull wits—there's shame therein;
There's shame in age save wits are keen.
Drivelling old age drives youth to laughter,
Nothing redeems that loss hereafter.
Nay, though old age be keen of wit,
Youth deems there is no sense in it.
Age joined with drivel—youth can see
Nought in them but stupidity.
This too hath age inborn with all
The rest: the more nonsensical
Its utterance be, the more aflame
With wit and sense it deems the same.
My master's words could well have proved,
Yes and his look, how far removed
From reason were my hopes—how oft
Would he dissuade me (but I scoffed)
From what he knew would harm. Alas,
Demented fool, blind that I was
To scorn his wisdom! One fine morning
Shall I be to my town returning,
Unchanged from what I was before.
Error that comes posterior
Is worse than prior—I portend
Much evil for my latter end!
The Mayor, Town Council, populace,
Will they not see me and my case
Discover? As he went out, they'll say,
So he's come back; nought new today.

True, if my tail were as it was—
But now they'll see what's come to pass,
And laugh and laugh; Mayor and folk
And Council all will see the joke.
If I was not before renowned,
I shall be now, and all around
Will point at me and mark me well.
Even where the cloister rules compel
To silence will the Brothers shout
(By fingers' aid) "His tail's been cut,"
And fingers will thus recompense
The loss of speech at my expense.
Best not return in this condition,
Until I gain a new position
To cover my delinquencies.
Hardy and firm my body is
As yet, and still (unless I lie)
I'm short of my centenary.
I'm brisk and brave and virtuous too,
But what to my dull wits is due
Is sharpening by mental work.
Nocturnal study I'll not shirk
Or fear to burn the midnight oil,
With head and body used to toil.
My age as yet is far behind
My father's; blows I do not mind,
Plenty I've had since boyhood's years;
I'm not a child to have such fears.
I shan't run home in downcast mood
Through scantiness of clothes or food.
I shan't play truant from my classes—
Too serious now to court the lasses;
And constant habit soon or late,
The burden will alleviate.
Nor, though I'm starting old to learn

What boys are used to, will I turn
In shame from study, neither fear
Will hinder me nor yet despair
From following out my fixed intent.
Two words give me encouragement:
Nought before constant toil can stand,
God helps the brave with His own hand.
To Paris then my way I'll make,
A ten years' course in Arts to take;
I'll start at once. Then, if God will,
I'll come back home, and, learning still,
Become well versed in all the rules,
By studying in Bologna's schools,
Of Civil Law; the Sacred Page
And the Decreta will engage
My final labours, if I live.
Then, then at last I shall receive
The title and reality
Of Master; Master shall I be,
And 'Master' shall precede my name.
If anyone omit the same
Before 'Burnel', that man shall I
Rate as the People's enemy.
Far shall my name be rumoured for
A peerless Public Orator;
People and Senate both shall crowd
To meet me, all shall cry aloud
'The Master comes.' By joint decree
Prelate and Brethren shall agree
To take my counsel as their own.
Stable shall be what in my town
I stablish, and what I decide
Shall with the force of Law abide.
What in my tail too short appears,
What over lengthy in my ears,

My name and honour shall redeem,
And gain than loss shall greater seem;
Reproach shall shrivel in the blaze
And glory of the latter days."

While thus he schemes, there joins him on the road
Another bound for Paris, with his load.
"Good-day," says Burnel, and with warm embrace
Inquires who, whence and whither he so must race.
"Sicilian I," says he "and Paris-ward
In eagerness for learning (God us guard
Upon the road!) I'm bound." "Three things we share,"
Said Burnel, "country, cause and that same prayer,

Our journey be the fourth! Now put your pack
Of books and boxes here upon my back."
So, joining hands in friendship, they proceed
In fellowship of heart and talk and speed
To Paris, and as they go the ass doth tell
His name and cause of journeying, how befell
Each happening, of the perils he endured,
How he left home and why, of Galen's word
And counsel given; then what Bicornis dared
To do, and how she and Brunetta fared
In change of season; how the Londoner,
One Trickman of Salerno, sold him there
Twice five glass jars, and how he lost them all
When Brother Fromund's mastiffs made him fall;
How the dogs died, how Fromund took his leap
And by God's justice due reward did reap;
The epitaph that on his tomb was writ,
And as for Paris, why he's seeking it.
So did he all his history unfold.
And when he'd done, Arnold this story told.

THE STORY OF THE COCKEREL'S REVENGE

The various turns of Fortune and of Fate
In human life 'twere hard to enumerate.
The vast events from causes small that spring
Stand plain to see, when facts fulfilment bring.
There happened in Apulia (some time since)
In William's day, the grandsire of our prince,
A memorable thing. A priest from town
Far in a country homestead settled down,
And year by year as e'er the time came round

41

Enjoyed rich harvest from his tended ground,
And by his wife had offspring, if to name
A married priest be lawful without shame.
Now of these children Gundulf was at home
Whom I once saw ere he to years had come,
He kept the grain and guarded the barn-door,
And often in his hand a staff he bore.
It happened once that Coppa with her train
Of chicks came pecking up the wheaten grain.
The hungry brood swarmed round the door, but he
With lifted stick struck out and made them flee.
He let his anger beyond limit grow,
Passing due measure with each word and blow.
When anger is immoderate, ere long
It borders madness; rushing into wrong,
All undiscerning of expedience
It wreaks injustice and gross violence.
One thoughtless throw—'tis made at heavy cost.
One thoughtless touch—some boon's for ever lost.
And as in too much wrath he plied his stick,
He broke the leg-bone of a cockerel chick.
Sore grieved the chick, sore grieved the mother hen;
Smarting in pain and shame, in anger then
He swore revenge. Time passed: the flesh grew sound
And firm; the new skin coated o'er the wound;
The broken bone has long its pain forgot,
But still the affronted heart forgetteth not
A scar without may still its curtain draw,
Yet in the heart within the wound is raw.
Long since the bone displaced is home again,
The mind remembering knows the exile's pain.
Foot firmly steps, no pain the thigh doth fret,
Shin feels no lesion, leg-bone's soundly set.
But still the mind limps, still the heart doth languish,
The soul complains, the spirit suffers anguish.

And, lacking which some hearts know peace no more,
Revenge expectant hovers at the door.
No rest for stricken hearts, no respite's aid,
While retribution tarries, long delayed.
No length of days brings respite to the soul,
Nought save revenge will make the sick heart whole.
Less keenly longs the dyver for its lake,
Less keen the wolf the fleeting lamb to take,
Or fish its stream or hawk its flying prey,
Than wounded heart a swift revenge to pay.
So too the cockerel was fain to see
Revenge, if chance allowed, for Gundulf's cruelty.

Six years had passed: the cockerel, now grown
A cock, performed the duties of his sire;
And Gundulf too grown tall claimed as his own
His father's living: such was his desire.
And nothing to his purpose now was needed
Save that the priestly office he obtain,
For to his prayers the bishop had acceded,
(Nor did blest Rufyn's merits plead in vain)
And for his consecration named a day,
The Sunday before Christmas, and the place
The town of Carabella. Proud and gay
Were Gundulf's parents at his happy case.
Before the holy day in preparation
Busying themselves a merry feast to make,
They send out far and wide an invitation,
Their house to all is opened for his sake.
Meats and rich dainties load the tables high,
And Bacchus streams in golden goblets rare,
To bless the house and cheer the company,
And all take freely of the lavish fare.
Now was the night when on the following morn
Gundulf should speed him to the appointed place

To be ordained; at cockcrow ere the dawn
Must he set forth, full many a mile to race.
The time, the hour prescribed the servants know
Whereat he must be summoned ere he start;
They must have care to hear the cock's first crow,
When herald of the morn he plays his part.
But when the vigilant cock of this did hear,
His heart was full of joy and jubilation,
Yet kept he silent; scarce could he forbear
From uttering all his heartfelt exultation.
Though to defer his joy was his intent
By keeping silence, yet the triumph song
Came nigh to bursting forth, impatient
Of further stay. Resentment stored so long
Bids him be mute, but joy would fain arouse
His chant, one prompts, the other checks; the scales
Between the two lie even; each he woos,
Yet will not; silence at the last prevails.
The guests at length (for now the morning light
Is near) wine-wearied take themselves to bed,
Nor reck they the divisions of the night,
So fast amid their drinking is it sped.
The night they cannot, though they fain would, stay,
Its wonted law they must themselves obey.
Meanwhile the time of crowing was at hand,
But from the songster comes no voice, no sound;
Silent are night and songster: servant-band
By night, sleep, wine in silence deep are bound.
The hen, long wondering that she did not hear
Her spouse and that his office was not done,
Softly approaching whispered in his ear
That time and hour were both now past and gone.
But "Vex me not, keep quiet," answered he,
"Stupid as ever! Leave me now, I pray!
Woe indeed for a wife's stupidity!

Sorrow will haunt that union, come what may."
Yet she as ever still importunate
Urged him to note the night's unchanging flow,
And he as ever striving to abate
Her wordy talk from prayers to threats doth go.
Then swearing still, that if he do not break
The silence, she will crow and waken all,
She waits no longer—a poor, scrannel squeak,
Comes forth, no more, a hoarse and grating call.
Yet one there was who heard and made reply:
"Hold your peace, Coppa, all in vain your noise,
No quicker comes the light to flood the sky
Because a hen has lifted up her voice."
Meanwhile night passes: drunkenness profound
Throughout the house holds all the company;
The cock sleeps too and in deep slumber drowned
Gundulf has dreams of pleasing phantasy.

Ordained a priest, he dreams, he's home again,
Donning his vestments, setting all in train
For holy rite. There in the Cantor's place
The cock he sees, in surplice trimmed with lace,
And hears him then with loud and raucous chant
Intone the Introit for the celebrant:
"All that Thou dost, O Lord, we ever see
With justice Thou hast done and righteously."
The chalice, large and filled with goodly wine
For due fulfillment of the rite divine,
He grasps, and swallows to the dregs, and then
Completes the office; but at closing, when
The Cantor to the people should intone
"Ite," no voice was heard, no sign was shown.
Then Gundulf woke and cried aghast in fear
With ringing voice, "Is day already here?"
He started up, but "Hold! no need to wake"

His servants cried "No signal yet doth make
The cock who knows and marks each passing phase
Of the long night, who, though we fain would laze
Through one more watch, chides us and makes us rise.
Better than we he knows how darkness flies,
How much is past, how much is yet to come.
Trust him, the unsleeping watchman of your home.
The night is long, the most part yet remains,
Turn yourself, sleep; a winter night contains
As much as three days' time, nor quickly wanes.
The trusty cock will keep us watchful, he
Although he wished could never silent be."
The cock thereat did whisper to his wife
"Yes, I'll go bail, you rogues! I'll stake my life!
Things take their course; 'tis as the coin's tossed.
Let sluggards tope, and topers pay the cost!"
While he thus spoke, the brilliant morn
Shines at each window; onward borne
Through every crack the light makes way,
And Phoebus floods the land with day.
By now the hind has yoked his team
And ploughs the vale. Roused from his dream
"Would I were dead at this moment" cries
Gundulf, and beats his breast and hies,
His breeches on the bed forgot,
In furious haste out to the stall
To saddle up; yet can he not
Rein, bit or saddle find, for all
Were changed about in last night's flurry;
No matter, halter in his hurry
For bridle serves. His haste's so pressing,
No time to seek a father's blessing.
Sped through the town in frenzied course

He's thrown and hits the ground; his horse
Strays off at random; he goes on
Afoot, but finds the service over,
The lads all priested, bishop gone,
No vacant place could he discover,
The reading's done, "tu autem" said,
And on the air the youthful Amens fade. . .
What can poor Gundulf do? No cure
But to go home. He must endure
Heartsick, the tears, the grief, the shame.
His parents, brethren, all aflame
With anguish mourn in sad despair;
The kinsfolk who had gathered there
Depart confused upon the morrow,
Seeing their joy all turned to sorrow.
Some blame the watch and some the drinking,
Says one, "No, 'tis the cock, I'm thinking."

When the hen heard these words she left her nest
And told the cock "Our Gundulf all distressed
And cheated of his priesthood back is come.
Deep grief and lamentation fill his home.
Had he been hangéd in a hempen cord,
They could not sorrow more, upon my word.
'Tis you they call plotter-in-chief and master
Of all this crime, main cause of his disaster."
" 'Tis no unfair revenge" the cock replied,
"But fair reprisal. Right is on my side.
I was — I well remember it — a chick,
When Gundulf broke my shinbone with his stick.
The cause and matter of my grief was he,
As evidence the fracture you could see.
He laughed at first, while still my wound did burn.

By just reprisal I laugh now in turn.
So Fortune plays her game of smile and frown.
Grief follows joy, things lofty topple down.
Relief of pain may come on lagging feet,

Yet when it comes, though late, is wondrous sweet.
Never too late the raw wound's medicines,
If they but cure the hurt, whate'er the means.
Easy reprisal, if no toil precede,
For suffered injury, is sweet indeed.
With no blood shed I triumph o'er my foe;
With no word said this joy my heart doth know.
Let others warfare make, my peace I hold;
Let bugles blare, my silence is pure gold.
The less the cost of triumph is to me,
So much more glorious is the victory.
No need of arms when silence wins the day;
Be mute, dissemble, that is wisdom's way.
Let tears in place of blood my foes outpour,
And anger thus requite the wounding sore.
For grief is the heart's wounding, inward pain
Sharper than outward sword can e'er attain.
External pains with healing soon pass over;
Hearts wounded scarce or never strength recover.
Far later injured hearts can solace feel
Than medicinal hands hurt limbs can heal."
Scarce had the cock thus spoken when death's doom
Laid Gundulf's sire and mother in the tomb.
His parents dead Gundulf from home is driven,
And all his father's house to strangers given.
Far from his home, with none to help him, poor,
Wretched, he begs his bread from door to door.
Yet many mindful how poor Gundulf fell
Did to their sons the doleful story tell,
That they might learn their passion's force to abate,
Nor know repentance only when too late.

While of such things still wayfaring they speak,
They come to Paris and there a hostel seek.
Weariness by repose is there made good,
And diet scant by lavish cups and food.
Tired bones, soiled skin, strained sinews, worn
    with toil
Of the long journey, are by baths and oil
Refreshed; and newly bled and with trimmed hair
Burnel, all combed and washed and dressed with care,
Goes forth into the town; he prays in church,
Then for which School will suit him best makes search.
And there with careful thought considering
The Englishmen, to them he fain would cling;
In wit and counsel shrewd, in courtliness
Pre-eminent, handsome, charming in address,
They rain their money on the folk, and hate
The skinflints; many a course in lordly state
Adorns their tables, wine abundant flows;
All this attracts, only three faults he knows;
But for these three all else would he commend;
They are "Wassail," "Drink health!" and "Lady
    friend."
Nor yet are these so reprehensible
That in due time and place they serve not well;
For two are banishers of grief and care,
And open wide the way to glad good cheer;
While the third takes the harm from violent passion
(Which, so we're told, in France is all the fashion).
So with the English would he comrade be,

And live like them in their own company;
Which he desires the more for having heard
In public talk of them a random word;
Company alters manners, and if so
Could not their company make something grow?
Nature to them past nature has been kind,
Why not to him — in front or else behind?
So with all zeal he buckles down to work,
To learn correctly and with taste to talk.
Alas, his wits are dull, his headpiece tough;
'Tis all in vain, he cannot learn the stuff.
Year after year passed by, the seventh now

Was near complete, but nothing yet, although
To teach him friends and masters laboured sore,
Had he contrived to say except hee-haw.
What Nature gave, what he brought with him there,
That has he, that can no-one from him tear.

At length his teachers, toiling hard and late,
Exhausted sank; the labour was too great.
Both rod and staff to Burnel's back and side,
And cane to hands, their labour bravely plied.
Now his ear's pulled and now his nose is tweaked,
A tooth's knocked out, a tender part is pricked.
He's cut, he's branded, bound and then unloosed,
Now thundering threats, now whining prayers are used.
Art in the fight petitions but must yield;
Nature commands, and fighting holds the field.
Where from the start a fault is deep inured,
Never or rarely can that fault be cured.

Hee-haw was early learnt: what else he tries
Like dust before the wind away it flies.
And now what is his case? the money's lost,
The wares as well and all the toil they cost.
No hope to get the tail he so desired,
Fair hopes but false the Englishmen inspired.

Then he, reflecting on the wasted days
Of youth and sadly self-accusing, says:
What life is this? What madness drove me here
Parisian schools and foreign lands to see?
What use to me is study year by year?
Was not Cremona good enough for me?
I left my homeland, crossed the Alpine range
In all its length, saw many a new domain
Far beyond Rhone; now in surroundings strange
(Poor fool!) at earth's far limit I remain.
What need had I at peril of my life
To see the Schools of Paris, and behold
The French, close-fisted, fosterers of strife,
The English, drunkards, lavish of their gold?
I came Italian, Frenchman I return,
Yet the same Burnel that I was of yore;
Nought to increase my knowledge can I learn;
Nay, I've forgotten what I knew before.
Could I but keep and speak one Frankish word,
Or two, 'twould surely admiration move;
Or three or even four — a thing unheard;
Like Jove I'd be or greater still than Jove.
Then Italy would know such panic fear,
The prince himself to me would tribute bring;
So not in vain would I have journeyed here,
If I could be my own land's sovereign king.
Far different is it now: far different
My hopes from what the Fates for me have spun;

53

A cruel lot has Fate upon me sent,
Ills plenty, but of blessings never one.
'Tis true indeed, for nowhere could you well
Find out a sounder or a hardier frame;
My feeling dull, like stone insensible,
My heart in hardness adamant would shame.
My brain, my head and breast are metal-hard,
And heavy, heavier e'en than lead are they;
Iron my legs, my side's an iron shard;
No single vein is in me, so I say.
My hide's like a bronze vessel, which in vain
You strike, no injury therefrom it knows;
No lashes kill nor malediction's bane,
Scarce could I die from heavy hammer-blows.
What happiness my mother then had known
If she had never born, or born me dead,
Or cut my young life short, or helpless, lone,
I'd been devoured by wolf that wandered
Into those parts! Why, often she would pray
He'd come and snatch me; surely I shall fall
His victim, for a mother's prayers, they say,
Find quick fulfillment so. Yet most of all
I feared when yesternight a dream I saw,
Which to me certain danger did foretell;
Methought my parents prayed: "From the wolf's maw
Lord, of Thy grace, protect our dear Burnel
And bring him home again; oh, safe and sound,
Untouched by lion or leopard, free from hand
Of peasant (horrid wretch!), from foreign ground
May he return to his own native land!
May he pass scatheless where the highroads meet,
All dogs be dumb, all slow to hear or catch
His scent, may wolves be gouty on their feet;
Ay, 'tis the wolf we fear so much; keep watch
We pray, on Burnel, bring him safely home."

And since by contraries dreams often go
I fear the more — for visions often come
Which from the day's fulfilment differ so
That they're explained by contrariety,
And if good visions come, then bad ensues,
If bad, contrariwise prosperity —
Such exposition did my mother use,
For knowing in such things she was and wise;
Much wordy warfare had she with my sire
Thereon, for that by contrarieties
They too did go: nor did they ever tire
Of sparring thus; her theories, he maintained,
Were false; for as a boy, in observation
And science of the stars he had been trained
And knew them all and their interpretation.
But whatsoe'er they thought, new fears o'erflow
My mind, I tremble; yet why should I fear
What must be, what elsewise can neither go
Nor stand — such fear lacks reason, for whate'er
Fate has decreed, will be; none can prevent
Or change or shun whate'er may be the will
Of Fate; who knows (not I) what will be sent?
A hard lot or an easy? good or ill?

BURNEL DREAMS OF BECOMING A BISHOP

Perchance the Fates have willed that I should be
In my own land a Bishop with a See.
More wondrous things are happening every day
Than that a bishop's rank I should display.
But should the garb of prelate me invest,
Where on my head will suit the mitre best?

55

For if my ears, as bishops', are held high,
The mitre cannot settle easily.
But though a prelate sign of office bear,
Power does not wholly in that badge inhere.
'Tis not the mitres that discriminate,
Nay, but the power that's their associate.
No mitre reft of pontiff's power shall gild
My head (if God to me assistance yield).
No mitre on my head, no horns for me,
If in their power be no reality.
Should mitre then lack power for my use,
A badge so sterile I must needs refuse.

A prelate shall I be full and entire,
Not as a mule I'll act, but as a sire.
Never would I an abbot's seal-ring hold,
His bogus mitre or his godless gold.
Never would I a sterile mitre take,
Which cannot the anointing power awake.
So bears a mule the limb of generation,
Yet ever lacks the power of procreation.
So they the emblems but no power possess,
They bear the name but yet are functionless.
Never for me such horns of high position,
The aim of this or that man's high ambition.
Full and entire must be my power pontific;
Not the name only but the thing specific.
Abbots can share with mules their discontent,
A fine display, but no accomplishment! -
By the cut mitre you may abbots know;
They're cut that they may ne'er to bishops grow;
Insignia lacking all substantiality,
Name ineffective, name without reality!
Burnel will no such title take, nor let
Horns without power upon his brow be set.
No guilt-stained hand, no gift by flattery won,
Or voice o'erquick to ask will Burnel own.
None will he let intrude him, give no bribe,
No compact base with Simon e'er subscribe.
He'll make no promise: prelates' minds should be
Sound but not seared, in conscience clear and free.
By neither prayer nor price, nor magnate's threat,
Shall Burnel come to his pontificate.
With single mind and clear I'll stake my stall,
Else bishop I shall never be at all.
With clergy's call and by due ordinance,
Lest I incur rebuke, I shall advance,
Lest, when this honour high has been conferred,

Some still may utter a reproachful word:
So did you climb, so were you forward thrust
By me, so, shepherd, entered on your trust.
For it you bargained such and such to me,
Your bond remember, to your actions see.
A bishop's life's a book, which all who can
Should read and mould their life upon the man.
A bishop's life should be a pattern true
To clergy and to faithful people too,
No vice, all virtue should be found in him,
That to his pattern they their lives may trim.
Nor lightly should he loose or lightly bind,
Fitting the power to avaricious mind.
Fair-spoken, single-minded, he should seem
Credit not debit in his folk's esteem.
Of his own goods he generously should give,
On no excuse his folk of theirs deprive.
Were his mind's eye not single, all his frame
Full dark would be, and all his life the same.
Even if in him alone the whole world's stuff
Of virtue lay, it scarce would be enough.
For who all things to all is bound to be,
Can he lack aught of virtuous quality?
Let no base cloud his inward vision dull,
Nor hate nor love his mental powers annul.
His duty let not flesh and blood make known,
Rather the Spirit's inspiration.
Let it not be that pull of fleshly love
Or headlong anger him to action move.
Let him the lame, the fallen, needy, blind
Their staff, their hope, their purse, their lantern find,
Th'accused his counsel; let him make his own
The widow's suffering and the poor man's groan,
The ward's sore need, and let him count as gain
What from his house the pauper has not ta'en,

Nor slight the poor, while their rich counterpart
He courts: man sees the face, but God the heart.
Let him not grasp as senseless worldly fame,
To please God, not the world, should be his aim.
Popular favour and short-lived renown
Is but a breeze that blows and then dies down.
To gain this favour, why despoil the poor
To make wealth wealthier than it was before?
To cram the rich man's maw with pauper's tears
'Tis hard to see what praise in that inheres.
'Tis wiser then, while there's a right to fame,
To spurn it than to buy at cost of shame.
For many who have courted present praise
Have won dishonour through unending days.
He who would curry favour in the eye
Of the vain world, that man acts foolishly.

So when I'm made the Bishop of my town,
In the whole world there'll be no rival known.
The people will come forth from every street,
And with bowed head their worthy Pastor greet.
What will my mother say, when in the press
She sees me both the folk and clergy bless?
She'll bless the day and hour she gave me birth,
And feel the happiest mother on this earth.
The honour will my father's heart rejoice,
When "father of our bishop" with one voice
And "master" too they call him. It may be
The rustic will be there the event to see;
He'll shake his head and mutter (none more shrewd
Than he from coast to coast):— "In my boyhood
Great things I saw, and greater ere I'm gone
I'll yet behold; now fortune shines upon
Burnel, it's his day now, as once it was
Another's; change abides, all else doth pass.

His very mother, who so despises now
The common sort, will surely once more bow
To bear her load; his father too the sack
Will bear again and now the title lack
Of "bishop's father"; yes, there's many a thing
I've seen and shall see; wrong to let it bring
Us worry or dismay." But this I fear,
And rightly; a small thing may yet cost dear.
The Prefect, save he be compelled, may not
Receive me in the city. This is what
Befell — God is my witness and the whole
City and countryside as well; he stole
A load of wheat-flour from my father's stall,
Where he and other two, citizens all,
In wicked, nightly theft had planned to meet
And steal whate'er they could; he took the wheat
Who is now city Prefect, one a horse,
And one a sheep. When ready now their course
Homeward, dispersing in swift flight, to take,
By chance or sound of feet the dogs they wake,
Who coming with my father barred the way.
So were they caught, and bound in prison lay.
Next morning, summoned to the market-place,
Came those who had decision in the case.
Holding their shameful burden stood the three,
The chains, whereof their hands and feet were free.
Fear for their deed and shame before their kin
Had kept them mute without and dazed within.
Though long denying they at last confessed
The guilt to all now plainly manifest.
The people's vote gave sentence they should die
By hanging — well deserved that penalty;
All night the servants ropes and wood were bringing
To make the gallows ready for their swinging,
When the compassion with me from the womb

Urged me to pity and avert their doom.
Yet did I not the common phrase forget:
Though you've a thousand enemies, he yet
Will be your bitterest who knows that he
But for your help a swinging corpse would be.
I knew it, but I heeded not: my heart
Drove me at last to play compassion's part.

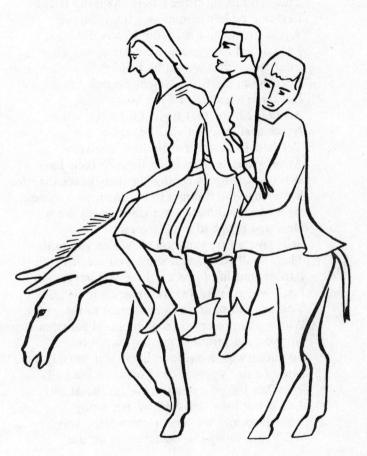

In secrecy I took my father's keys,
Then loosed their chains and gave the rogues release.
Alone, at night, unwitnessed (lest if known
The crime should bring me punishment) — alone
I dared this splendid deed of bravery,
Whose memory in my mind will never die.
So they escaped the halter and the rack
Through me; all three I bore upon my back,
Lest one be left behind or witness know,
'Cross stream and road and byway did I go.
I've carried heavy loads, but know not when
I carried such a weight as I did then.
Each by himself had weight enough for me,
But three together! if I live to be
A hundred, for that night I'll be the worse;
Never shall I forget that deadly course.
Yet had I rather save the unfortunates
At my expense than leave them to their fates.
And they, when weeping on their knees they fell,
Scarce had the strength to bid their ass farewell:
"Lo! Master Burnel, your three slaves are we,
Here and now and to all eternity.
Sell, give away, summon us where you will,
There shall we go and show you service still,
Pardon and life to us all three you gave;
Each will remain for evermore your slave,
Yours in full right, in rightest right to use,
Whom you preserved from gaol and hangman's noose.
Are you not lord and master evermore
To those whom on your back you bravely bore?
Must he not yours indeed his own life call,
Who but for you would have no life at all?
And if our lives last shall we not repay
Your help and toil in a right worthy way?
We'll sure repay the debt before we die,

The Lord so grant us opportunity."
How often did they to the ground incline
Their heads, assuring me that they were mine!
Then, lest my sire should know what I had done
And all the city too, when they were gone
I took their chains and swore, a heavenly stroke
(Forgive me, Heaven!) each single fetter broke,
And that Saint Leonard came, the prisoners freed
And took their chains away. Now for this deed
I fear the Prefect will make recompense
According to the saying, in converse sense,
With evil treatment my good act requite
And as inferior show me harsh despite.
Yet I should not despair nor suffer fear
(Since myself too the guilt of crime must bear)
If in the wretch a drop I could espy,
A single drop of generosity.
For generous natures render good for good,
But currish spite and sour ingratitude
Are powerful, nor can doctor's skill suppress
Or cure the taint of servile churlishness.

BURNEL LEAVES PARIS

Thus pondering he's determined quite
To leave the town by morning's light
Next day, he bids his comrades all
Farewell, and while the teardrops fall
He's off, away and hurrying fast,
When on a hill he halts at last,
And lo! spread out before him lies
The city lately left; he cries

Amazed: "By Christ and Sainte Marie,
What place down yonder do I see?
Surely 'tis Rome, of cities all
The greatest, with its circling wall
And rising towers; and here above
What other than the Mount of Jove
Can be this height? Then in what land
Am I? Is Rome so near at hand?
But sure 'tis like the city where
I lately studied — ah, I fear
The name is gone, quite lost, alack!
What was it? — no, it won't come back.
To think that when my parents say
What was your town, where you did stay?
I can't recall a town so famous!
They'll call me cheat and ignoramus,
And blame me for the money lost.
So back I'll go, and at all cost
The name recover, lest at home
I'm called a blockhead when I come.
Then if I can but prove I know
The names of places, that will show
I've kept my terms and been at school,
If not, they'll laugh and call me fool,
They won't believe a word I say."
While, eager to retrace his way,
He thus reflects, a countryman
Comes up and asks, "What do you plan
To do in Paris? teach or learn?"
Paris — now he can once more turn,
He's caught the name, and in his head
Must keep it, never lose the thread,
Through chance or wish for conversation,
Else he'll renew the situation.
Nothing but "Paris" on his tongue,

Except for "Paris" all day long
For fifteen days, whate'er his wishes,
He'll be as dumb as any fish is,
Whoe'er salutes, whate'er befall,
He won't reply or speak at all.

For full twelve days Burnel his vow
Religiously had kept, and now
There came a pilgrim bound for Rome
(Vienne near Lyons was his home)
Who in mid Alpine region meeting
Drew nigh and gave him kindly greeting:
"The Lord be with you, reverend sir,
Morning be kind and evening clear!
Good fortune all the hours of light,
Good lodging then and quiet night!"
But Burnel, as he onward stept,
His self-appointed silence kept,
Nor made reply, no single word,
Only by signs he showed he'd heard
The word of greeting, bowing low.
Together then the two did go
Into a hostel, on their bed
The long way's weariness to shed.
And since his friend, devoutly praying,
His Pater Noster oft was saying,
Burnel, awake, cried out: "Alas,
My word is gone, the word that was
My only word is vanished quite,
The pilgrim praying in the night
Filched it away; that syllable,
So like the word I knew so well,
That Pa Pa Pa so oft repeated
Has my poor word, alas, defeated.
Ah well, I've often heard it spoken,

65

'Tis better compacts should be broken
Than with a faithless partner made;
And I by this unwilling trade
Of word for alien word have squandered
My seven years' toil (this, while it pondered,
My true prophetic mind foresaw).
In its first syllable, no more,
My word was like to his, the end
Was different; which, could I but bend
My memory to grasp, then Jove
Would to me far inferior prove.
Indeed I'd give a hundred pound,
Or e'en a thousand, were I found
So rich, that this ability
I might possess; but 'tis gone by;
Scarce that first syllable I own,
But all the rest is lost and gone.
Still, something's better far than nought,
And I shall cling to what I've got.
Part for the whole, the learned say,
Enough for me, will it but stay.
Whole, one part lost, no more survives;
Whole, one part staying, partly lives.
Keep of the whole one part, 'tis better
Than to keep nought, not even a letter.
Many to keep I was not able,
But many gone, yet one thing's stable.
One syllable of a seven-fold Art
Is something, ay no feeble part.
Since knowledge, ofttimes fostering lies,
Puffs up o'ermuch its votaries,
To shun the lapse and loss, I see
One syllable's enough for me.
Overmuch knowledge tedium brings,
And documents are wearying things.

Nature exerts her power best
In small things, ev'n the tiniest.
Shortness of studies brings more pleasure,
The spirit's harmed by lack of leisure.
Many collect mere scraps of learning,
And hope that they much fame are earning.
Much toil there is in knowledge, gaining,
Teaching, in memory retaining.
But be it clever as it may,

Knowledge can never teach away
Death, whereof all men stand in fear,
Both one and all and everywhere,
Death by a stern, impartial Heaven
To all in equal portion given.
Death must I fear, lest ere I know
He come and say " 'Tis time to go."

BURNEL DECIDES TO ENTER THE RELIGIOUS LIFE

Why, then, to save my soul, I'll enter on
The life religious, and the time that's gone,
My youth, let age redeem; I'll strictly check
My life, that what remains may not to wreck
And dismal ruin slide; for all offence
And shameful error I'll show penitence,
And better late than never; a good end
I fain would make; if cloud the morn attend,
Even if the whole day into cloud be thrown.
Let a clear evening for dark day atone.
What Youth has wasted undiscerningly,
Prodigal in its flower and vanity,
Let fruitful Age, rich in experience,
For wastages of Youth make recompense.
Hope flowered, but flower withered, hope declined
From hope; that withering, fruit's no more to find.
All hope of flower is gone, in fruit alone,
While hope remains, can aught of use be shown.
Death, that's so sure, most secretly doth hide;
From all concealed to all it's open wide.
Death is to all a communal possession,

Whereto has each in turn his own succession.
What can more public, more private be
Than death, of all, of each the property?
What do I here then? how long do I stay
In service of the world? Why any day
Death, saying Here am I, rise up and go,
May be at hand. What then am I to do,
Save only to the cloister's life depart?
So let there be no tarrying ere I start.

BURNEL CONSIDERS THE DIFFERENT ORDERS:
THE TEMPLARS

But many Orders nowadays I see,
Nor am I clear which would be best for me.
If as a Templar I the Red Cross take,
They'll sure dispatch me overseas, to make
Payment of vows, and somewhere far away
Near Tyre perhaps, I'll slave and slave all day.
Yet I'll not go on foot, a horse I'll ride
Wheat-fed and fat, easy to turn and guide
With touch of heel, sure-footed, ambling slow
With easy motion (for the Rule says so:
The Rule forbids to ride a trotting horse;
Through me that rule will never lose its force!)
I'd like to join the ranks of white-coat men
And fight, but I should ne'er come back again.
For the infidel will slaughter me, then flay
My hide right off, and fling the rest away.
The wolves will have their fill, and my poor skin
Will furnish leather straps for Saladin.

THE HOSPITALLERS

Or should I then the White Cross emblem don
As Hospitaller? off to Lebanon
Shall I be sent; there dragging many a load
Of wood I'll groan beneath a three-pronged goad.
Belly will empty be and basket too.
Though much I'd like to say, nought that is true
Will be allowed, but only boasting lies
That magnify the House; if once or twice
I break the rule, "Out, out with you" they'll say,
"Get out from here," and tear the cross away.

THE CLUNIACS

If I should take a robe that's black,
And live and die a Cluniac,
On eggs and beans and salt I'll sup;
At midnight, though, they'll wake me up
And turn me out of bed when I
Would go on sleeping cosily.
What's even worse, they'll make me chant
From tonic up to dominant;
My voice is loud enough in tone,
Although a little hoarse, I own;
But coughs and a congested chest
Will make it hard to sing my best.
If I won't sing, then I must be
Lamp-bearer to the company,
And wait till morn for my reward.

Often on Fridays at their board
Will meat and fats be seen, for there
That is permitted. Coats they wear
Of leather, fur-lined; and yet more
They keep concealed in private store
Secret from their companions' gaze;
For of those folk and all their ways
Not even the lord abbots learn
For all their will and precept stern.
Breaches of ordered silence bring
Rebukes that wound and blows that sting;
And should I strike through wrath or wine
I'll suffer punishment condign,
Even, they say, imprisonment.
To outside places none are sent
Save those who've worked both hard and long
The cloistered company among.
No priories are bought or sold
Nor other lands; nothing for gold
Is given; kinship cannot stand
Nor Abbot's friendship 'gainst the band
Of cloister brethren; nor will they
From Rule or morals any day
Be led to suffer dispensation.
If from the monkish corporation
A cloud arises, sure the Head
Will see that it no further spread.

THE CISTERCIANS

As a White Monk, on common fare I'd mess,
But they provide two well-cooked relishes.
They hate, what I have ever sorely hated,

71

A peasant's holding near their own located.
They lust for land, these plaguy folk, and groan
If neighbours' fields set limits to their own.
Enough of milk and wool their beasts provide,
But with enough they're never satisfied.
Always encroaching, though their needs are scant,
Had they the world, they still would be in want.
They'll feed me well while I'm a novice yet,
But keep me busy, for to all are set
Their special tasks, lest any seem to be
Slothful, or lacking share in industry.
A sabbath-rest is rare, for with less work
There's less to eat — good reason not to shirk.
The rod's in frequent use, the diet's rough;
Unappetizing fare's thought good enough.
Never flesh-meat, save one in high position,
Abbot or Prior, kindly gives permission.
Strong meat of four-foot beasts the Rule denies;
So flesh of bird that runs or bird that flies
They long for, not as tasty but as rare.
But when they cook it, no-one dwelling near
Perceives the smoke, too conscious of the act.
The meal all done, no vestige of the fact
Remains, for lest the chicken-bones be found
Crying "We're here" they're buried underground.
To all are given three tunics as by right,
Two cowls and a short scapular — by night
No drawers impede them as they lie in bed,
No fear lest I be thus inhibted.
No measure mete you'd wish not to be meted
To your own self; treat as you would be treated.
True brotherhood in act not name we see
Name without deed is unreality.
Many there are by wrongful name alone
Termed brethren, yet to us as hostile known.

Paul of false brethren in his works has told,
Through whom he suffered perils manifold.
Real are the perils that false brethren bring,
Many, nay all our ills from them do spring.
Each of his brother should beware, nor place
Or hope or faith in him; a faithless race
The brethren: though one trusty be, no less,
Winning no trust he's lost trustworthiness.
They cozen and are cozened each and all,
Brother carnal and brother spiritual.
Should you a truly faithful brother find,
Make him the half of all your heart and mind.
So many false, so many feigned are they,
So many fierce — their number none can say.
Who in the cloister are no more of right
Than Satan is in Heav'n — such things affright
My soul, toward Religion while I tend,
Nor clearly see my journey nor its end.
Perhaps my fears are vain; oft is it so
That hearts of men unreal terrors know.

THE GRANDIMONTANES

Should I profess the life and take
The robe of Grammont, they will make
Things harder far for me, I fear.
Though they own nothing, nor can bear
That aught by any owned should be,
This nothing gives sufficiency.
Their cloisters are remote, they keep
No silences, their fingers sleep
For tongues are free; no pasture land,

Estates or farms do they demand.
Their wool not ten sacks full provides
Each year, and all from breast and sides
And neck must in the same sack go;
No difference in the wool they know;
Neither do they the bare pelts tan,
Stripped of the fleece. The brothers man
No fishing-boats, with rod and line
Or nets to catch their prey. No swine
In woodland do they fatten up.
If well or frugally they sup,
What things they eat or when, to me
Must e'er remain a mystery.
But if their food like manna rains
From heaven, no need of more domains.
By nature and condition men
Not angels are they, wherefore then
Debar them from what men desire,
And alien ways of life require?
What's done in secret rarely fails
To stir suspicion, though the tales
Of wrong be false; did they but aim
The stubborn power of flesh to tame,
'Twere better far; yet I herein
Make no reproach and find no sin;
A servant must, as saith St. Paul,
To his own master stand or fall.
With quarrels and with suits at law
They vex the public courts, and draw
To endless length a trivial case.
Though they be poor they spend apace;
For fifteen years the case goes on,
Long buried in oblivion.
Both hard and long they strive, and spend
Their money vainly without end.

Divided are they; for the priest
Performs his office at behest
Of the lay-brothers there; the Mount
Was troubled sore on this account
And journeyed Rome-ward; even so
No end can their disputings show.
They've shed much wealth, but like a well
Is Grammont, inexhaustible,
And all their needs in wondrous wise
Unsown, unploughed, unreaped supplies.
Why, if within the cloister ground
Men of angelic lives are found,
Should they so oft be thrust about
And jostled in the world without?

THE CARTHUSIANS

Should I to some Carthusian cloister go,
More leather coats and tunics they can show.
I'll have a cell all to myself alone;
No comrade and no servant shall I own.
Alone I'll sing, alone I'll take my meal,
Alone at night my way to bed I'll feel.
My triple cell will ever me immure,
Nor shall I put one foot outside the door.
To cook my meals there'll always be a share
Of greens, of firewood and of water there.
There will the Prior visit me, and oft
A large loaf I shall have, that's warm and soft.
A fixed share they for sustenance receive
Of all that earth and sheep and cattle give
And woodland; by rough goatshair shirts they seek

To mortify the flesh; three times a week
Their fare is bread and water; never fish
Except on feast-days only; when they wish
Or have the time, they can hear Mass of right
Once in a month or twice. Contented quite
With their own goods, neither to rich nor poor
A burden would they be. A canon sure
Rules of what lands or herds they are possessed,
Nor may the number ever be increased.
From flesh for ever are they all debarred,
Save him whom wasting leprosy hath scarred.
Their feuds to settle they make no resort
To public justice, neither do they court
The empty greetings of the multitude.
Whene'er a guest arrives, with change of food
They welcome him, and what they have impart
With cheerfulness of voice and hand and heart.

THE AUGUSTINIANS

Good is the life of the Black Canons too,
Worthy and godlike, in the people's view.
Soft things they wear, and fats and meat consume
(Though wine's forbidden) in their Dining-room.
How has meat sinned, though green things have
    no blame,
That it should not be eaten just the same?
No guilt in meat: 'tis he must guilty plead,
Who eats unwisely nor restrains his greed.
Though wine's accused, the toper blame must take,
If in the morning head and body ache.
Lest tedium come from psalm or lesson long,

They're moderate both in reading and in song.
Nor do they in their tones all measure lack,
Nor bawl as though the roofbeams they would crack.
Pure for the pure, a habit clean and white,
Of linen woven fine, is their delight.
It lacks all roughness, keeping in its use
With skin and flesh an honourable truce.
Black is the outer robe they wear; for so
Some meaning do the alternate colours show.
The blackness dims the force of dazzling white,
In darkling fear refulgent joy shines bright.
So in the rainbow double splendours shine,
So in the leopard dark and light combine.
So black and white the magpie's feathers share,
And crows among the black white feathers bear.
Thus garments double-hued the flesh adorn,
But not the heart; by it no stain is borne.
Only the robes doth stain of black demean;
What matter then what colours there are seen,
If no conflicting hues possess the heart,
But single-hued it rules the inward part?

THE PREMONSTRATENSIANS

The brethren of Prémontré go
In gleaming habits white as snow;
White sheep's wool only do we see;
They please by their simplicity.
Soft garb at present they refuse,
And rough they've chosen for their use.
Roughness of wool will castigate
The flesh, lest it luxuriate:

The wether's crisp and curly hair
Or, where the neck would else be bare,
That portion of the fleece they take.
Yet has the Order for their sake,
Since linen is prohibited,
Prescribed the softer wool instead.
Great is the Rule's austerity
Which bans in perpetuity
Meat from the brothers' table, yet
The Order has upon them set
A lighter burden, doth dispense
Herein more wisely — no offence
To lie in fats of meat, though lean
Shall on their table ne'er be seen.
At war with flesh, with fats they show
Their love of peace, and will it so
That flesh's honour be maintained
Nor by unjust decisions stained.
For flesh if wholly banished might
Of injury complain by right;
Yet if received without condition
Might oft do mischief on admission.
So stands the cause of flesh in doubt,
Not quite let in nor quite put out,
Partly admitted, partly banned,
An exile in its native land.

THE SECULAR CANONS

Canons we also see called Secular:
Yes, Canons of the world in truth they are.
Pleasures both law and license to them give,

Such is the Rule by which those Canons live.
Nothing do these despise or e'er refuse
Which panders to the body and its use.
But this chief principle have they laid down,
Which to all ages all their like must own:
Each man may have one woman (saith the law),
But now each man may have one woman — more.
These eagerly the world's fair blossom cherish,
And keep it watered lest it fade and perish.
These in all things with petulant flesh comply,
That to their sins an open road may lie.
These show the way whereby with headlong speed
They the whole world to utter ruin lead.
These men are not the world's, the world is theirs,
And urged by them to sheer destruction fares.
These undermine the Faith: deep is the breach
Between their lives and what in words they preach.
Through these the vigor, power and influence
Of Church and Bishops wanes and loses sense.
Through these respect for Clergy is decayed,
Nor any honour to Religion paid.
Through these men kings unrighteous plots unfold,
And weakly loose what they should firmly hold.
On the left hand of kings and pontiffs set
False tongues they are, hands eager but to get:
A double heart, a love that meets no test,
Bottomless purse, brigandage unconfessed,
Name without power, foot erring from the path,
Feigned quiet, real motion, latent wrath,
A balance false to truth and true to guile,
Fore-running cause of ill, page rich in wile,
Fame that's but dirt, a life that is but toil,
A path that's ever set on slippery soil,
Law without God, Rule without Christ the Lord,
Their fate's unsure, but grief's their sure reward.

Their tongues they've taught to lie; they sell for gold
Pure justice undefiled; while they would hold
The falling world from ruin, in its fall
They lose their hold, its ruin whelms them all.
Yet some of them there are who in their heart
Reflecting strive to keep themselves apart.
These have the world abandoned, flower and grass;
The world with them doth now for nothing pass.
As in the fire where the Three Brothers met
Their contest in a ring of flame is set.
Yet are they scatheless: fire can work no harm
Against the Spirit's cool refreshing balm.
The world's their furnace: as the gold thereby
Is prov'n, so God refines their quality.
Scatheless to lie in midst of flames and fires
Surpasses Nature and God's work requires.
With one's own flesh to battle hard and long
Is a hard task and fearsome, for to wrong
Man's flesh is prone and soft as wax to sway,
Where sin ingrained in nature leads the way.

THE HOLY NUNS

The Order of veiled women too we know,
Or holy nuns: by that name too they go;
Unmarried girls and widows joined in one—
The Order is by now to many known.
They keep in wonted manner, one and all,
By night and day the hours canonical.
In high-pitched tones they chant, so sweetly ringing,
You'd surely think that they were Sirens singing.
Slender in form as serpents they appear,

The serpent's wisdom in their hearts they bear.
Deft like Susanna in the face-cream's use,
Sirens to sing, like Paris amorous.
Yet one thing all the rest doth countervail,
Their tears that stream 'fore Heaven without fail.
Appeasement and forgiveness thus they win,
By these they purge and cleanse whate'er their sin.
Far as their ears they let their tresses grow,
The Rule forbids that they should further go.
Black gowns they use and unshorn lambskins white;
Black hoods cover their heads; away from sight
The sable habits veil the whiteness chaste
Of limbs that lurk within; around the waist
They wear no girdles. Quarrels are not known,
Save circumstance compel or reason shown;
Nor do they strike, save urgent cause be there.
Barren are some, and others children bear,
Yet all are virgin called; most fertile she,
Whoe'er is deemed to bear most worthily
The pastoral staff; scarce one is barren found,
Till age itself to bearing sets a bound.

THE GILBERTINES

Now a new Order has appeared,
Lately in our own country reared,
Which (for it is a good creation)
Shall have a good commemoration.
From where it grew it takes its name;
They call it that of Simplingham.
Simplingham from simplicity
(If not by contrariety)

Is named. One house in fourfold wise
Arranged hold two societies,
Of men and women — Canons here
And laymen too, and Sisters there,
As many. Duties they divide,
Canons say Mass, and on their side
(For a high wall is set between)
The Sisters by the men unseen
The other Offices attend,
But not unheard; their voices blend:
Intoning without melody
They speak the words continuously.

BURNEL'S NEW ORDER

While on all this I silently reflect,
I'm at a loss which Order to select.
Safer and wiser will it be, I trow,
To constitute a brand-new Order now,
And write its laws; its name my name shall be,
Name that shall live to all eternity.
This is the way: I'll from each Order choose
Whate'er is best and suited to my use.
First from the Templars nags that amble well,
So that my Rule may comfort to me spell.
This from the Hospital would I retain,
Where'er I am to lie with might and main.
The Cluniacs from their Rule will this provide,
That fats and meats on Fridays be supplied.
This boon from Cîteaux shall I borrow, which is
That during night-time I dispense with breeches.
I praise the Grandimontanes in one matter

Which I would keep, that is, their endless chatter.
Like the Carthusians I shall be precise
That every month one Mass alone suffice.
With the Black Canons let us meat permit,
For none shall brand me as a hypocrite.
We'll imitate the wise Premonstratensians
In tunics soft and gowns of wide dimensions.
The one Rule left decrees a lady friend
Be joined to me by bond that knows no end.
This rule was at the first by God's behest
In Paradise laid down and by Him blest.
This rule my ordinance shall aye maintain,
For of this Order were my parents twain,
Yes, all my forebears too; and if this fail
Nothing to save mankind can e'er avail.
From the veiled women's holy Rule I choose
That I henceforth no more a girdle use.
Broad girths I like not, tight ones even less,
They do not suit my belly's ampleness.
Another thing they have, which I'd transplant
To my own Order, should occasion grant.
From Simplingham — their novelty is such
I'm doubtful what to borrow or how much;
But this on no account will I omit;
Essential to my folk I reckon it;
That never save in secret, all beside
Unknowing, shall a sister e'er abide
With any brother. Some things else there be,
Forgotten now, but time will easily
Call them to mind; so nought now doth remain
Save confirmation from the Pope to gain,
Which he will gladly give; for never they
Have found that the Lord Pontiff said them nay
Who just petitions make. So now must I
Far hence upon my Romeward journey hie,

To press my suit, and with submission meet
The Pope and all his brethren to entreat.

BURNEL MEETS GALEN ONCE MORE

While thus he planned, came Galen travelling,
And saw him and drew near and welcoming
Said "Are you not the Burnel that we knew?"
"Indeed I am," said he; "greeting to you,
Dear Master; I am Burnel from your town;
You will remember me, I was well known
To you, once young and brisk and strong,
Now broken down by ten years' labour long.
I have had miseries countless, there's no doubt;
But one thing sapped my strength and wore me out,
The School's exhausting toil. Yes, torments two,
Inward and outward, vex me through and through;
The rustic goads and beats me, tears my skin,
The School devours my very heart within.
Rather would I 'neath heavy mill-stones bend
Than every night in constant studying spend.
Hard lot indeed! yet what the Fates have spun
I neither can come short of nor outrun.

BURNEL DEPLORES THE CORRUPTION OF THE
ROMAN COURT

Sorrow and doubt in turn my heart assail;
Dispirited my spirit's like to fail.

Scandals so dire, so numerous abound;
Princes and prelates both are guilty found,
And wicked deeds, too foul for me to tell,
In Church and State cause harm irreparable.
When weeping this poor world I contemplate,
Its past, its present and its future state,
Like snow and ice from the sun's presence flying,
Or wax at fiery impact liquefying,
I faint, I fail and scarce in body stay,
But fountain-like pass into tears away.
Whereof the chief, the cause especial is
The Roman Curia and its policies;
Rome, sovereign queen of princes, coronet
Most brilliant upon brows of rulers set,
The City's glory and the world's, the day's
Bright shining beam, the night's carbuncle blaze,
Hammer of wrong, quick punisher of ill,
Sharp sword of justice, pity's flowing rill,
Bloom ever fresh that never heat could stale,
Unfailing fount, balm dropping without fail,
Religion's citadel, the warrant sure
Of peace, the generous hand that helped the poor,
A nation's banner, rule of righteousness,
The torch of faith, of wrong the sure redress.
She, once that Way whereon all men were led,
Should be again, as once she was, their Head.
But now, turned back, her word she's lost to mind,
And what was head before is tail behind.
Once, without stint and lavishly, to save
Her own, herself and her own blood she gave.
But now conversely is she different grown,
To shed another's blood she drinks her own,
And sheds unstinting and with ostentation;

'Tis death she brings who should have
    brought salvation.
The contents of her cups she has transferred,
And labelled honey what's with poison smeared.
Yet her own throat still rages without cease,
A thirst no drinking ever can appease.
That mouth wide open, though a mighty sea
Of gold flowed in, would never sated be;
Its greed no meats, its thirst no goblets quell.
Woe to that maw, that pit insatiable,
Whose avarice not ev'n a world can fill,
Whom her own plenty makes a beggar still!
The poor man sins and for his sins must pay,
The rich man's money purges his away.
A purse well filled will set the guilty free,
Empty it sets the good in jeopardy.
No task so hard, no crime so grave or base,
A well filled purse will remedy the case.
License she'll give to whatsoe'er gives pleasure,
And take from lawful things in equal measure.
Others' offence she cleanses, not her own,
Her wounds remain unseen to her alone.
So ailing head fills all the limbs with pain,
A little poison spacious jars doth stain.
Plague from one sheep to a whole flock can pass,
A little blemish spoil a mighty mass.
So tastes a stream of its far distant spring,
So smells the smoke from a fire's smoldering.
From the head's illness all the body ails,
A parent's sin his progeny bewails.
The Glory of the virtues, the world's Head
Is Head of all its vices now instead.
Nay, had I all the years that Nestor knew,

I could not tell all that to tell is due.
But now to sum and 'neath one term to lay
The People's voice (the voice of God, they say)
In all that frame nothing at all that's sound
From crown of head to sole of foot is found.

BURNEL ON PRINCES

Yet should I now the ways of princes prove,
Ev'n greater wrath and sorrow will they move.
Harsh are their lives, their rule but sternness knows.
Their words are but a breeze that lightly blows.
And man, though in his Maker's image made
Who all, that is, created, yet is paid
By princes less regard than beasts of earth,
Ay, all our race is held of lesser worth.
How many are hanged on cruel gallows-tree
For taking flesh of beasts! more savagely
Sicilian tyrants could not well ordain
Than that for slaying beasts a man be slain.
So do they rule, captains without a crew,
Scarce only is the name of kings their due.
Although affrighted lands they subject hold
And from their folk gain tribute of much gold,
These do not rule, for ruling does not lie
In being feared or in harsh stringency
Of laws; not Rulers should we title them
But Robbers: from their acts the name doth stem.
No truth is in them, trusting in their ways
Folly, nay madness, in my view betrays.
Their tongue is full of guile, their hands of blood,
Their ways are faithless; active to no good

Save for rewards are they, and so employed
Justice and judgment leave them null and void.
For all they do and meditate and say
All smells of money, if due heed you pay.
Gifts must go fore or after or near to,
Like calf to cow, whate'er you wish to do.
No rank or habit else, no reputation,
No title wins from them consideration.
Gifts can excite or smooth a monarch's frown,
Gifts can bring peace and then again bring war,
Gifts bring both kings and prelates tumbling down,
Gifts make and then unmake both right and law.
Gifts give persuasion to the tongues of fools,
Gifts cry aloud and then all else is mute,
Gifts flout decrees and break established rules
And tear ancestral rights up from the root.
Gifts lend a charm to great men's wicked ways,
And screen ill deeds that they may more abound,
Gifts—but my tongue no secrets here betrays—
In holy hands, alas, are ofttimes found.
Gifts clearly show what greedy men devise,
And all the guilty longings of the mind;
Gifts manifest their power when empty lies
A bishop's seat—this often do I find.
Gifts a sweet poison that sound hearts can cure,
But death's own living image to the weak,
Gifts have a power of utterance, strange but sure,
And for the mouth, though it be silent, speak.
Gifts, when a judgment's in the balance, tip
The scale to where the money makes the weight,
Gifts are a deadly venom to the lip,
And blind the sight and drive too fast the gait.
Love conquers all, but gifts can conquer love;
You doubt it? balance both together well.
Gifts choke the seeds of good, incitements prove

To saints, drag sinners down to lowest hell.
Gifts raise a prelate, raise a monarch high,
Confer distinctions, hearten chiefs of war.
Gifts corrupt morals, ruin chastity,
Suitors desire them at the harlot's door.
Gifts undermine the loftiest towers, level
Mountains with valleys, work a bloodless death;
Gifts go before, and in their train the devil;
When gifts appear, the cause lies close beneath.
If gifts should cease, we'd see an end to strife,
Mars ruined, Venus left without a friend;
If gifts should cease, without expense of life
(What ne'er befell) great Rome would meet her end.
If gifts should cease, then primates' palls will be
Cheaper in value and of lighter weight,
If gifts should cease, then abbots too will see
Their horns decline in people's estimate.
If gifts should cease, back from the royal Hall
The monk will to his holy cloister go;
If gifts should cease, then flock and shepherd, all
In spirit one, true peace at last will know.
If gifts should cease, then back to Cluny's cell
Will God return, perhaps, and there abide;
If gifts should cease, the clergy will repel
Simon the Mage and Judas from their side.
If gifts should cease, at last the whole world through
Will be an end of anger, grief and brawl;
If gifts should cease, Judas and Simon too
Will lose their power and money-bags withal.
See how the untaught, lawless populace
Rush blood-stained on to every foul excess!
How folk whom lust for flesh and blood doth fill
Arm innocent hands for every deed of ill!
Once did they fear the Lord, both monarchs, yea
And people too; gone is that fear today.

Why speak of God, who we no longer heed?
Each is his own; of other there's no need.
Sheep follows sheep, so do the folk their king.
In violence and folly wantoning.
Ruin on ruin marks the'unhappy time,
Day after day brings crime to follow crime.
None to redeem or save doth now remain;
What once we hoped would save, is gone nor comes
    again.

ON SPIRITUAL PASTORS

Who bears the blame for all this wickedness?
The holy pastors of these days, I guess.
Who claim as prelates to uphold the law
Yet in their lives their own commands ignore.
Thieves and not pastors were the fitter name;
The holy page bears witness of the same:
"Many false prophets shall be spread abroad,
Eager on many hearts to work their fraud.
And though as innocent sheep they're clad, yet know
Like ravening wolves they wander to and fro."
Those men the name of shepherd rightly keep,
Who feed, not feed upon, their helpless sheep;
But these their functions have inverted quite,
Nor guard like shepherds but like wolves affright.
For three there are who near the fold are found,
Shepherd, hired man, and wolf that hovers round.
One feeds the flock for nought, for hire the next,
But by the third 'tis ravished and sore vext.
Our pastors, then, since nought for nought they give,
Can with the first claim no prerogative;

And since for hire they serve, so with the second
In likeness of their work must they be reckoned.
Of shepherd nought, of hireling much they own,
But for the wolf their case is plainly shown.
For wolf-like come the pastors of this age,
Subjecting each his flock to brigandage.
Like wolves, of flesh and blood they make their fare,
Ev'n from the mother's womb the offspring tear.

What's weak they spurn, what's frail they crush
    and slay,
What's fat they eat, what's poor they fling away.
For milk and wool they harry and divide
The wretched flock, and drive it far and wide.
Nor think enough the fold to violate,
And for themselves its wealth to appropriate,
But the poor creatures' lifeblood must they shed,
And glut their thirst as warm it flows and red.

How they intrude, the shepherds of these days,
Into the pens, how led and by what ways,
How they behave once there, what zeal they show,
Trust the world's voice, not mine, if you would know.
Probe well our pastors' lives, and you will find
How much to blush at! to their faults they're blind,
Though full exposed to view, where all around
Can see, as though uplifted from the ground.
Themselves and their own folk in every need
They care for; flesh and blood they ever heed.
But whom they should promote—how hard his doom,
Scarce has he power to keep the lowest room!
Sores, fever, hunger, thirst and want beset
Him by whose toils our daily bread we get.
But at the prelate's board how gay the scene!
How many courses borne along! what sheen
Of flagons, goblets, cups innumerable!
How many different wines there's none can tell.
Seneschals too and servitors yet more,
Boys that stand still and boys that pace the floor,
Youths trimmed, beribboned, decked in varying wise,
And old men telling older histories.
As in a royal camp dispersing go
The guards, so briskly run they to and fro.
While their lord drinks, lo! one on bended knee
Does homage, arms outstretched, adoringly.
Throughout the Hall both gold and silver shine
(Wherewith the sacred Host in rite divine
Is offered), ay, no cheap or worthless stuff
Is for the pontiff's use good enough.
How sinful an apportionment, to choose
Pewter for God's, but gold for prelate's use!
Silver and gold to grace the pontiff's board,
When churches scarce can earthenware afford,
When empty churches see their altars bare,

Their crosses stripped of spoils once blazing there.
The prelate's hall inside and out soars high
On stately columns' marble masonry.
Who knows how many capes his wardrobe swell?
Mantles and cloaks has he uncountable.
The prelate's fingers shine with gems and gold,
Which seven rich men would wealth sufficient hold.
He runs through marks (not Mark) at rapid pace,
And Luke to lucre takes a hinder place.
So what's on trust, not given them, they dispense,
While God maintains His long indifference.
How and to whom they give (their gravest task
Of all) the cure of souls—no need to ask!
While yet the baby in his cradle lies,
Nor calls by name but only wails and cries,
Ere he can stand or walk, 'tis on his knees
Lie care of souls and wielding of the keys.
But what will Peter say when Robbikin
Takes me with him to heaven, or Willemin?
'Twas Peter and no babe to whom the Lord
Trusted the Church's keys in watch and ward.
Save me from Robby and Willy, Lord, this day;
Let me not fall into their hands, I pray.
But I'll not fall, unless (Lord grant he mayn't!)
The bishop force me to by hard constraint.
If so, I'll make appeal and go on foot
To Peter and his heirs to plead my suit.
Then Robby with his nurse will go there too,
Borne in a covered basket old or new,
And Willy in a handbag will be brought,
And be received by all the Roman Court.
Nor empty-handed will they come, or spare,
But like a woman near her time to bear.
They will draw nigh and see the famous tomb,
Which large and empty has capacious room.

What's lacking in their years will he supply
By influence who bears them company.
Father and pedagogue will lend their years
All they require, if need for that appears.
Who churches gave, did he not years bestow,
And such behaviour as such folk should show?
He who gave one thing sure the rest could give,
In all he owned the same prerogative.
Boys we have seen, who've not yet grown a beard,
Pastors of churches, even to sees preferred.
Of such a one, when once a king essayed
To make him prelate, 'twas in answer said:
"A prelate? but we cannot yet make out
Whether 'tis boy or girl; there's still a doubt."
Such are they who in God's house rule today,
Whom folk and clergy too must needs obey.
Such are the pillars that Christ's Church do prop
Till weakened ere its time it needs must drop.
You ask what is our busy prelate doing
Here in the town; with all his dogs he's going
Off to the woods and fields, perhaps to see
His birds bring down their quarry, or maybe
To cast a hook for fishes, and belike
Draw out a perch or a voracious pike.
A heron near the river bank is spied:
Straightway from town the bishop forth has hied
To fly his falcon; oftener he is found
In woodland glens than treading holy ground.
A wounded dog or injured falcon grieve him
Far more than should a single cleric leave him.
Whole days are wasted oft in endless pleas;
A short hour's ample for the Offices.
Long hours consumed in argument seem brief;
A short hour's service bores beyond relief.
Hounds after hare with more persistence run

Knowing no respite till their task be done,
Than prelates of our day, at season due
And hour, will read the Sacred Office through.
If they endured for God what they endure
For worthless ends and delights unsure,
Who would not deem them, yet alive on earth,
True Saints, with Martyrs sharing equal worth?
And yet no shame or penitence they feel,
Although the yoke they bear leaves many a weal;
Their God for whom they suffer present woe
Will for their merits due reward bestow.

ON ABBOTS AND PRIORS

Abbots and Priors (stranger still to tell)
And holy Convents whom their rules compel
Reject the Canons which they've vowed to hold,
Which holy Fathers made for them of old;
And now, like dogs to vomit, they return,
Or sow to filthy wallowing, nor spurn
What they've once spewed; they keep a holy face,
But in their hearts guile only has a place,
And be they Benedict's or Bernard's folk
Or subject to Augustine's milder yoke,
Under whatever sacred sign they claim
To magnify the Lord, all are the same,
All thieves; trust not their words, their raiment white,
Scarce even their actions trust beyond your sight.
Their voice has Jacob's smoothness, but elsewhere,
Neck, hands and arms are rough as Esau's hair.
So back to Egypt where the fleshpots call,
With none restraining rush they one and all.

Drawn by the flesh they fall into the pit;
Pharaoh's oppression—why, they welcome it.
Keen envy stings, and strong ambition plies
A triple goad to their activities.
Self-seeking first, and next, unsleeping zeal,
Unthinking love, which they for kindred feel;
This fiery plague, with which they all are cursed.
Puts God to second place and holds the first.
Then, to gain wealth there's nought they will not do,
And what they quickly grasp they ne'er let go.
Once to be poor and lack the goods that pass,
The wealth that fades, the greatest glory was
Of the religious; now, save they possess,
Imperilling their souls, no small excess
Of wealth in flocks and herds, in field and mead,
They deem themselves unfortunate indeed.
For to be thought a poor man in these days
Involves, they hold, a criminal's disgrace.
Christ was a poor man, whom they imitate
By being poor—in name but not estate.
So what they'd fain be called they'd fain not be,
And think to cheat the all-seeing Deity.
They've given up all, and vowed in utmost need
The path of Christ to trace—in word not deed.
They've scorned the world, yet so that once resigned
It's yet at hand, so oft they have the mind.
That nought be lacking, all things they've disdained;
Happy, who little sowed and tenfold gained!
The wolf in sheep's garb unsuspected goes,
But by his savage bite can fear impose.
The fox moves quietly with modest mien,
Wherein no reason for mistrust is seen;
But far beyond all beasts his heart is sly
And ever first in guile and treachery.
The loftier the flight the falcon makes,

The nearer to the sky the course he takes,
With mightier swoop he falls upon his prey.
The ram, that he may butt more fiercely, may
Retire a space but then with head bent down
He takes the other's blow and gives his own.
Thus is the world induced these folks to deem
Worthy of praise and even as saints esteem.
Much more remains to say, yet more I fear
To speak just now, lest blame I needs must bear.
But what of the lay people? Ah, I'll be,
If I say all I know, a Public Enemy!

BURNEL OVERHEARS A DISCUSSION AMONG THE BIRDS

Once from the city in hot haste I ran,
When from my master I would fain be fled;
Bernard was he, that wretched countryman,
Whose cruel blows I ever held in dread;
I sought some place which he'd be sore bestéd
To find, but with his dogs he followed fast,
And many an angry threat on me he cast.

Through all the byways on my track he came,
Swearing that if he captured me, my hide
Should pay full dearly and my guilt proclaim
By script whose markings would so long abide
That I should ne'er forget it; once he tried
And thought in savage glee with thrust of arm
To take me as I groaned, but out of harm

I leapt and mocked old Bernard as I went;
Then with my hooves I struck him, and he learned,

Flung on his back, to groan for my content.
Now was I weary, and the sun's heat burned,
And safe beneath an oaktree's shade I yearned
To rest, and there my ditties to indite,
Which to compose was lately my delight.

Suited for writing were both time and place;
No need to urge me; tired were my feet,
My belly full; ready whereon to trace
My verses, as was due, in fair and neat
Inscription, lay the lambskin parchment-sheet,
And as my hand lifted the sharpened pen,
High in the branches of the oak just then

I heard a sound of chattering, and straightway
Of flying, fluttering birds so vast a brood
Filled all the place with noise of chirping gay
That, wide and spacious as it was, the wood
Seemed strait and narrow through their multitude;
With voices manifold the air was riven,
They shook the ground and echoed back to heaven.

In fear I to myself began to moan:
"What is this strange event?" and all afraid
Through solitude and the wild wood unknown,
Unmoving but with ears erect I prayed
Prostrate for mercy, but with no sound made,
And beat my breast, and (did I dream it so?)
Much water in my fright from me did flow.

So when strong winds and angry tempests roar,
It only needs that a few raindrops fall,
Soon are they quiet and heard no more.
Then in the wood the clamour and the brawl
Died down, and sudden silence fell on all
At once; alone the raven from the throng

Arising spoke the listening birds among:

THE RAVEN

"Dear brethren all and masters of my kind,
Hear if it please you, not that I in worth
Surpass you or in wisdom of the mind
Excel or in nobility of birth,

Sprung as I am but from a clod of earth;
And wisdom its beginning hath in fear
Of God, as we from mighty David hear;

Nay, but because as tale of years can show
Older than any of you all am I;
Wise Noah made me in his ark to go,
At seven years old, when the great flood rose high
And scarce could one the mountain tops descry;
Since when of many times I've taken heed,
Known but to few, but happy times indeed.

Which when I silently recall and think
How good they were, how full of sweet delight,
Comparing with our present case I sink
In sorrow and despair lest the dark night
Of death fast hurrying overwhelm us quite;
The glory of the world is passed away;
Nor earth nor sea their ancient laws obey,

Nor stars in heaven their wonted tenour keep;
Disorder reigns, e'en night and day their name
Disown in deed, and Nature holding cheap
Her own decrees fights Nature; with its frame
No limb coheres; no age remains the same
As that preceding, one day to the next
The world is different; so are we vext,

Both men and beasts, by ailment and by pest,
Birds languish soon and die; the cause is plain,
We have all sinned, and none his guilt confest.
'I have done nought, nor I, nor you, no stain
Of guilt in him at all,' we say: 'in vain
You blame us' say the servants everyone,
'We took no drop,' yet all the drink is gone.

And though one were resolved a full admission
Of all his sins and evil deeds to make,
With tears and sorrow and with deep contrition,
And pardon humbly beg for mercy's sake,
Whom could he for a safe confessor take,
Secure of silence? none of us, I trow,
Nor could I any of my tribe (although

In thousands fathers, mothers I can rate,
Brothers and sisters too) as counsellor.
For if I told the crow, he'd tell his mate,
And she'd proclaim my sins from door to door;
Or if the cock, his henbird all the more
(Which God forbid!) a gruesome tale would spin,
And tell her chicks how great a rogue I've been!

Take warning, then; as my black feathers prove
My garrulous tongue once brought sore harm to me.
While I was silent, happiness and love
Of friends I knew and all prosperity;
Then, uncontrolled, my tongue's loquacity
(A curse on it!) changed former love to hate,
And stole me from my true and better state.

Happy, had I some shape of Mars in stone
Out-silenced, and my whiteness still were left;
But now my once-committed sin I moan
For ever, and what then from me was reft,
Grace, beauty, fame, whereof my tongue too deft
Deprived me; 'twas my tongue that wrought me ill;
Silent, I had retained those blessings still.

Of all most fair was I, to all most dear
Among the birds; my voice, so rough today
'Tis scarce a voice, of yore was ringing clear

101

(Of my sad crime another witness); nay,
My fame had shone with never-failing ray
Had I been silent; through the word I said
My fame is all to nothing vanishéd.

Be warned of me, then, and your tongues restrain,
Lest madly they to your destruction race.
Now by my masters' leave some truths I'd fain
In briefness speak, if here for truth be place.
If oft we find ourselves in evil case,
No wonder, in ourselves the reason lies,
If such we seek, of our adversities.

To all the cornfields we destruction bring,
Ravage sown seed, and crops in early blade
Or teeming harvest rob; scarce burgeoning,
The blossom lest it come to fruit we raid
With tearing beak and rending talons' aid;
Constant in harm and rapine, slow to good
Are we, a selfish, greedy multitude.

His grain now threshed, the peasant thinks, is stored
All safely in a well-fenced granary;
Now comes the cock with all his hungry horde,
They peck their fill and soon away they fly;
Nor are content to take sufficiency,
But with their feet must scatter the whole mass
About the barn, wherever they may pass.

The hawk and falcon, though with plenty fed,
Fly off, nor deign their master to come near,
And vainly doth the lad his arms outspread,
Calling them back and shedding many a tear;
They scorn the friendly hand that used to bear,

That used so oft to feed them: ev'n as though
They'd been long time in thraldom to a foe.

And though the lads pursue them in their flight
At imminent risk of death, by stream and wood,
And ofttimes die pursuing, yet their plight
They pity not at all; thus we in feud
Against our friends much evil give for good.
The parrot next, too slow his mouth to close,
Nor gift of speech nor gift of silence shows;

For oft when maids with timid whisperings
To faithful ears and honest witnesses
Have aught revealed, he to their mistress brings
Their secrets, soon as she returnéd is
Back to their chamber; hence conspiracies
Whereby to poison us maids often seek,
That we may die ere we can learn to speak.

And other birds there are, who never stray
From sacred cloister and its broad estate;
How often they each year on many a day
Work harm I cannot here enumerate.
For these misdoings we incur the hate
Of angry men, who thus for our offence
With stern reprisal wreak due recompense.

Hence daily snares and gins for us they set,
Limed branches trap us, held by foot or wing,
We fall unwary in the extended net,
Or quickly die by arrow-shot or sling,
Or captive to the flute's sweet carolling;
And thus our sins, inept and needless shown,
By just requital must we needs atone."

THE COCK'S REPLY

While yet the raven speaks the cock replies:
"Enough, my friend, cease, curb your vain expense
Of words, unskilful as they are unwise;
I like them not, more sound have they than sense,
Like an old man's prating eloquence.
Your tongue, it seems, aforetime worked you ill,
Yet you learnt nothing, it is harmful still.

Much you have seen, like one who long has lived
And many ages holds in retrospect;
No wonder then that soon of wits deprived
You drivel like a dotard, whom defect
Of mind and body doth at last subject
To chance not reason; for when reason fails
No limb, nor tongue nor eye nor hand, avails.

Hence your rebuke of crime, your accusation,
As though in goodness none with you could vie;
For sure you won the whole world's admiration,
As Noah's Ark itself can testify!
For Noah, when away he bade you fly,
Expected your return—what kept you there
Upon the hill? a carrion corpse, I swear.

So belly's pleasure and gross appetite
Induced you then your master to betray.
And just as gluttony and base delight
In carrion taught you treason, so today
Now you are old you cannot put away

That faithlessness; yes, faithless you'll remain;
What childhood learns old age must needs retain.

How different am I, how different
From yours do all my ways and deeds appear!
Whoe'er my master, all my life is spent
For him in faithful service; every year
With comforts rich and poor alike I cheer;
On my soft feathers weary eyelids close,
Their strength renewing weary limbs repose.

Most do we aid the doctor's healing art,
Food suited to their case to sick men give,
Delicate meat that brings to better heart
Such as are weak or ev'n despair to live;
Fat gelded capons healthy folk receive.
From us too come the eggs (so prized they are)
'Gainst which the cloister monks wage truceless war.

More vigilant watch than any guard I keep,
I mark night's passage with my chant till day,
Rouse lazy lads who fain would longer sleep,
Nor suffer them in cosy couch to stay;
More benefits I bring than aught I may
Recount to you, nor would I service slow
Or heart ungrateful to my master show.

And if I wished to vent my spleen, and set
No check upon my tongue (which God forbid)
Many for crimes would justly pay the debt
High on the gallows or in prison hid;
Ay, many live of whom we would be rid,
Both men and women, if the world but knew,
As I myself know, what they dared to do.

Deeds nightly done, deeds blacker than black night,
I could recount; such things I know and hear,
A master's act, a servant's word of spite,
What a shrewd peasant whispers in the ear
Of his shrewd wife: may never Chanticleer
(So grant it, Heaven) the base informer play,
And use his voice to injure or betray!

No, may I never play the Raven's part,
Of his preserver once the treacherous foe,
May Jupiter ere that with fiery dart
Consume me, or the earth in caverns low
O'erwhelm with all my race, or torrent's flow
Submerge me deep; no, may I at the last
Into the black abyss of hell be cast,

Ere the entrusted secret I should tell,
Or ever to base word my tongue give birth;
For who with others must together dwell,
Unless he love them and commend their worth
With praise and honour, as a clod of earth
Must witless ever and unfeeling live;
His body feels, his heart's insensitive,

Such is my mind, my true opinion,
Which for myself to you I here declare;
Let Hawk and Falcon testify their own,
And all with years and utterance to spare.
By fate the rule of country folk I bear,
Far from the Court, nor ever entrance make
Save when I'm trussed upon a wooden stake.

But Hawk and Falcon live in castles proud,
And share the counsellings of royalty

In secret places where the noisy crowd
Of common folk is silenced; set on high
Much in the king's own chamber they espy;
The farthest corner, apt for deeds of night
And secrecy, to them belongs by right.

Here many a wicked plan is formed, and here
Are evil schemes attempted; youth and maid
Prefer dim alcoves to the daylight clear
Of the wide hall; here in its dimmest shade
That which has issued from the womb is laid,
Brought out before its time; here is confessed
What never priest did hear, and what were best

He should not! Here by patient search obtained
Are deadly poisons stored; with all their power
Here stepdames ply their spells; on mission feigned
His ailing falcon in its hidden bower
The youth must needs seek out at midnight's hour;
Asthma and falling sickness here are healed,
And oft must daylight to the darkness yield.

Such are these places which detest the light,
And hold high value from the traffic base;
The falcon and the hawk can judge aright,
Frequenting many a far from holy place;
They know why thus I speak, and that the case
Thus lies; those two, if they but wished, could tell
Of happenings strange but true, as they know well."

THE HAWK

"To shun one's duty wickedness I deem,"
Replied the hawk; "of noble race am I,
Of stock unblemished; it would ill beseem
My mouth to utter words of villainy.
Let lads do what they will; continually
Let us bear with them, let them have their sport,
To do them harm is madness, in my thought,

When they have not harmed us. They are not slow
Their secrets in our presence to confess;
Justice constrains us therefore not to show
Their guilt abroad. Besides, they bring our mess
And meal, these lads, and with all carefulness
Look after us; they take us with the men
Out to the fields and bring us back again.

Just hatred does the base informer reap,
A crime it is a friend to incriminate,
Eyes see surprising things, yet silence keep,
So why should tongue what ne'er it saw relate?
And Heaven forbid that tongue collaborate
With eyes in such a way that harm befall
Both from one only; wherefore keep in thrall

Two eyes when mouth, that is but one, for harm
Is given release? The mouth then silent make
Till ears and eyes can speak, and leg and arm;
Then tongue at last imposed constraint can break
When other parts the power of utterance take;
So soon as ears their hearing speak, and eyes
Their seeing, and the hand and foot likewise,

Then will the tongue once more its vigour loose
On those who caused this question — though be sure,
If for itself and fellow limbs its use
Bring harm, it must in silence yet endure
Till it has learnt due caution to secure.
For of all vices which the world infest
This wicked vice is far the wickedest."

While thus the hawk was speaking, slumber sheer
Fell on me and my drowsy eyelids bound;
I slept, and sleeping snored out loud and clear,

As is my fashion. By the sudden sound
Alarmed, the birds from all the woodland round
Scattered more swiftly than a breeze in spring,
And brought an end to all the parleying.

Such thoughts, dear doctor, oft as I recall,
Grave cares distress me and my heart appall.
Nothing beneath the sun stays fast, we know,
Nothing is stable, all is flux and flow.
Lo I, who once was young and brisk and bold,
Patient of toil, am broken now and old;
And though my years past ninety sure have mounted
Scarce three days, as it seems, have I yet counted.
By all I see the grave alone is left,
Ev'n one day more is soon of light bereft.
To wish long living is (which Heaven forfend!)
To wish long sinning; so let life soon end.
Since from the womb no day can sinless be
For any child—how shall it stand with me
Who fear not man, and God but little heed,
In sin abide nor e'er repent my deed;
Nor sin unknowing, but in wilfulness;
Do ill aforethought, full of wickedness;
Sinning in thought and word and act—still worse
And worse from day to day becomes my course.
Bad yesterday, today more wicked grown,
Tomorrow wickedest shall I be shown!
Where is this leading me, to every evil prone?

So for the life religious am I now
Determined—into which, if God allow,
Soon as may be I'll enter, for to me
Declining years bring sore anxiety.
Doctor and Founder of an Order new
To Rome I hasten, confirmation due

110

To gain; a willing Court I hope to find,
Nor will the Pope, I fancy, be unkind.
Now, Master, should you wish your life to change,
Take my advice, no further need you range.
Before your pupil have no shame to kneel
For the Lord's sake and for your own true weal.
For in Religion this we often see:
The lesser rules, the great must servant be;
What's worthy to unworthiness yields room,
Roses 'neath thorns, lilies 'neath thistles bloom;
Freeborn to slave, wise man to dolt gives way,
Just to unjust and light to night's dark sway.
So be not vexed: what useless is or base
With the more zeal men set in highest place,

And put in practice thus a tale of old,
Which by my mother oft to me was told.

THE STORY OF THE THREE SISTER FATES

Three Sisters on a kindly errand went
(Goddesses they, whom Fates we sometimes name),
Relief of human care was their intent,
One purpose in all three alike the same;
To mend the faults of Nature did they aim,

Where she had lavished bounties in excess,
Or else withheld from oversparingness.

So journeying, upon a wooded mound
A girl of noble birth and beauty rare,
Of beauty matching nobleness, they found,
Worthy the bed of Jove. For one so fair
Once seen the gods had surely vowed to bear
Arms against Jove; and he a seven years' space
On earth had dwelt, to gain that girl's embrace,

Out-cast from heaven. Nature no richer cream
Of beauty could have given, had she been sprung
Of Jove himself, or by the Stygian stream
Had sworn; yet ever now her head she hung,
And wept and made lament, and ever wrung
Her hands and rent her cheeks and beat her breast;
Her tears made wet the ground her footsteps prest.

Two Sisters seeing her were fain to go
And help, and urged their comrade to bring aid
And cause at least a lessening of her woe;
But she with word and look refusal made
And deaf to all their sore entreaty stayed;
But lest they feel distressed or timorous
Or slighted by her words, she answered thus:

"You know the purpose of our coming here,
To succor folk — but only those in need;
She needs no help, this maiden, for whoe'er
By Nature to her utmost hath indeed
Been blest, as she, by gift of noble breed
And peerless form—for her they should suffice,
These gifts, both in her own and in our eyes.

Help if we gave might hurt; increase ere this
Hath many harmed, for whom it had been best
To live content with their simplicities,
Nor for unlawful things indulge a zest,
Or strive beyond the powers they have confessed.
What tallies not with Nature's work and will
Soon fails and falters; Nature heareth still

Reason, not force, nor can she long endure
That contraries together should unite."
The goddess spoke, and going would not cure

114

The girl's distress, but left her in sad plight
And still lamenting. Now the fervent might
Of the hot sun and labour of the way
Pressed hard upon the goddesses, and they

Wishing to slake their thirst at a cold spring
Sought near at hand a grove's refreshing shade;
Scarce had they reached the place, when, wondering,
Alone upon a couch a fair girl laid
They saw; she with glad smile to rise essayed,
But could not move her limbs; no power had she,
Save to stretch out her arms to greet the Three.

She taught them then the ways about the grove,
Where the pure stream came gushing from the ground,
And said "How gladly with you would I rove,
Did Fate allow; but to my couch I'm bound,
A grievous deadweight doth my limbs impound
Continually; but lately was I brought,
And left alone here in this shady spot."

Then the two Sisters when they heard her tale
Wept, and long time their leader did implore
And try with prayers and weeping to prevail
That to the girl she should again restore
Her power to walk, on her own feet once more
To stand, to leave her bed no longer stay.
But she unmoved, unpitying went her way.

"I see" she said "that as is meet and right
Pity constrains you; your desires I know,
Kind are they but unjust, so in despite
Of reason they must suffer overthrow
In justice name. This girl for whom you so

Implore me lies, I grant, confined to bed;
Her legs are weighted down as 'twere with lead.

Yet in her other limbs much vigour lies
And many special gifts therein combined,
Take but account of her abilities,
A voice both strong and clear, perceiving mind,
Her handiwork could scarce an equal find
For beauty; in three things she doth excel,
In mind, voice, hand, and fair is she as well.

Let that suffice for her; in craft of hand
She by herself is of ten girls the peer.
Why lies she thus alone then? the command
Of Nature hath enriched her so, 'tis clear
We need not lavish further bounty here.
If in this one thing—lameness—she doth ail,
In three, ay four, see how her gifts prevail."

Hearing her words the Sisters now did cease
Their tears, and hastened to pursue their way;
But evening prompted them to gain release
That night can bring from labours of the day;
So at the entrance to a town which lay
Hard by they sat, now ready to compose
Their limbs to slumber and their eyelids close.

Lo, from the town a country maiden came
To ease her belly, where the roads divide;
Before the heavenly ones she showed no shame;
Up went her skirts, nor cared she aught to hide,
Then bent her knees and squatting down did bide.
One hand a crust held, one a wisp of grass,
Each duly doing service to the lass.

Nor for the passing folk did she give over,
Nor for the goddesses who lay near by,
Of whom two blushing must their faces cover
With garments lifted, and attempt to fly;
But the third stood and checked them with her cry;
"Stop, what has done you harm? Come back again;
What do you fear? Your fancies are in vain.

'Twas but a gleam you saw low in the sky.
What this poor maid to us so clearly showed,
Was all she could, in her simplicity;
Had Nature but a kinder lot bestowed,
The new moon would not so for us have glowed.
No sparing then, but pity and quick aid
In her distress! let lavish gifts be made

And bounty show'red upon her. Nought hath she
Of Nature's giving, spite of Nature's store.
We must bring succor; she in penury
Abides and needs our aid; nor ever more
Could rise by her own power, nor if she saw
Ruin, could any help but we alone;
Nothing for her avails that is her own.

Nature hath made her poor and destitute
Of inborn grace; only the powers that lie
In Nature's gift not Fortune's bear the fruit
Of riches, and contain their augury;
'Gainst Nature no such power can we supply.
Nor do we (what can ne'er befall) design
That through us Nature's vigour should decline.

What once was nature nought can ever change
Without or yet within; but outer state
Of wealth and living can we rearrange,

Nor harm what Nature as her own doth rate.
Justice and Reason shall to us dictate.
So then let us to whom the power belongs
Make to this lass requital for her wrongs.

With lavish hand let us our gifts bestow,
Estates and revenues of wealth untold,
Pastures and mountain-granges, herds that low
And bleating flocks and spreading fields to hold,
And, among other honours manifold,
Grant her as Queen this city to possess,
That nought be missing from our bounteouness."

This tale I often heard my mother tell,
Nor blush that I remember it so well.
Such in religion too is oft the way;
Much happens wherein reason wields no sway.
Such is the life within the cloister gate,
And such, dear master, oft will be your fate.
A wide-spread fault—with it are many cursed,
Many indeed—and prelates are the worst.
Hence strains and stresses spring, and so we find
Pastor and flock are oft of different mind.
Hence in religion grave disorders meet,
Scandals and schisms, loss, contempt, deceit.
Virtue, which oft attacked can much abide,
Her eyes from scorn and slighting cannot hide.
No hurt so keen, no sword-stroke bites so nigh,
As when despised and slighted virtues lie.
For other agonies with time may wane,
This festering in the heart must e'er remain.
This wound doth ever spite of med'cine grow,
This ulcer worsens still as time doth flow.
Snake-poison thus is dropped into the wound,
Venom for which no antidote is found.

He who when scorned can patiently endure
Can against other wounds remain secure.
Patience triumphant other ills defies,
But 'neath this weight alone defeated lies."

While yet he spoke, from his left nostril gushing
Cold blood in short and sudden spurt came rushing.
Then said Burnel: "Something unfavourable
This sign portends to me. I mind me well
This happened on the night before that day
When the four mastiffs bit my tail away.
May this blood be for good, if but the Lord
Avert the omen, and success afford!
To those who wish me ill may running hare
And limping she-goat their own omens bear,
In morning met; may they in morning's hour
See first the owl, that bird of evil power.
A barefoot woman spinning wool black-hued
With distaff fashioned from the yew-tree's wood,
At morn an aged bald-head and at eve
A tousled bent old crone may they perceive
As they go walking, or a voiceless monk
Of either colour, head on chest down sunk,
Or angry priest late come from funeral
Of pauper or of widow to them call,
Or toad in all his body manifest
Cross leftward on their path, or that worst pest
Of all (as people say, and sure 'tis so)
The rustic meet them whe'er they go!"

Scarce had he said these words when in there came
The dour old rustic—Bernard was his name;
He shut the door and said: "What, Burnel here?
I'm Bernard, your old master; many a year
I've searched for you, and by a lucky chance
I've found you; now you'll pay for all that dance
You led me, I can tell you. Come to me,
Come, Burnel; back to town where treacherously
You fled we'll go together. 'Twas at night,
One Sunday at New Year, if I am right,
You dared that crime; and since you got away
There's twenty years gone over, I should say.
Now old and broken, all your vigour gone,
May God forbid you should go working on,
Unless compelled or of your own free will,
If the work's easy—just the daily drill
You know so well, that's all you'll have to do,
A few cut logs to carry, and my two
Panniers, of course, and two wheatsacks beside,
And me on top—no great weight, sure—to ride."
With that he threw the halter o'er his head
In the old way, and home poor Burnel led,
With cudgel showing him the way to take;
And lest once more a crafty bid he make
For flight and freedom, as he did before,
And from his master his due toil withdraw,
Old Bernard cut off both his ears, that he
Might learn some caution from his cautery.
"Now do I know for sure" remarked Burnel,

"Since head and tail at last agree so well,
What truth that holy prophet did declare
Long since in Paris, when I studied there.
Oft did he tell me of the future, clear
As 'twere the past (I cannot tell it here).
Whate'er he said had been or was to be,
What came to pass confirmed his prophecy.
Much too of you he spoke and much foretold
I'll ne'er forget, nor do his words grow old
And fall to ground unmeaning. Often too
Would he discourse of all that he foreknew
Would come to me; five times unfortunate
I'd be, and then five times a lucky fate
Enjoy. Now of these five misfortunes four
Are passed, and so there but remains one more,
The fifth and last, which now I undergo,
The term and final end of all my woe,
For this last plague will bring me to my goal,
Repose from toil, the longing of my soul.
Now the misfortunes five are overcome,
Five blessings wait for me in equal sum.
This wicked countryman my plagues began,
And so they'll end, with this same countryman.
From boyhood's days my foe, the primal cause
Of ill, stubborn and obstinate he was.
He questioned first my status 'fore the law
Who never had been aught but free before.
His cunning brought me into servile state,
And made me bear these burdens' heavy weight.
But now by change of fortune my vexation
Just where it first began shall have cessation.
Not I, in truth, that cruel rustic, he
Was the first cause of my adversity.
So due requital for his cruelties—
Therein no wrong, nay pious duty lies.

121

Give limb for limb, the ancient law doth say,
And tooth for tooth and foot for foot repay.
So will I do to Bernard, unless Fate
(Which God forbid!) far otherwise dictate.
Oh if the future he could see, and know
What glory on Burnel it will bestow!
He would not ply so hard his staff and rod
Nor prod my side with iron-pointed goad,
Nay rather on his knees would venerate
My footsteps, and my favour supplicate."
Amid such thoughts and dreams Burnel has come
Back to Cremona's city, his old home.
He enters by the gate, and there once more
Lives subject to his master, as before.

THE STORY OF BERNARD AND THE
THREE GRATEFUL BEASTS

A strange adventure Bernard now befell,
Whereof Cremona's city oft doth tell.
For people's talk lets not past history fade,
To past time's weakness ready to bring aid.
Thus people's talk renews that feeble state,
And will old histories rejuvenate.
The loss that years, that dying ages bring
It thus redeems, past deeds exhibiting.
Three children Bernard had to feed at home,
His wife made four, a donkey fifth did come.
This ass, though small and frail, was prop and stay
Of Bernard's house and household, many a day
He carried logs to market, and all five

Alone by his sole labour kept alive.
Now once when Bernard to the woods had gone
Out from the town with his companion,
He seemed to hear a voice that cried "Save, save!"
Muffled, as though it issued from a cave.
He stopped, amazed, and on his forehead drew
The cross's sacred sign, then listening knew
It was a man's, that bitter cry of fear.
Marking the region whence the voice most clear

Upon the air came winging, he pursues
A quick path thitherward. So sound gives news
Of voice, and voice of word, till of the word
The voice makes clear the meaning; thus he heard:
A rich and powerful lord, Dryane by name,
Who from the city of Cremona came,
While hunting in the woodland, as it happed,
Had fall'n into a pit, and there was trapped.
Narrow was it at top, but broad below
And deep and dark, and in had fall'n also
A lion, an ape, a serpent; Dryane, he
Made fourth in most unwilling company.
All four were frightened and all four were dumb
Save him whose fright caused cries for help to come
From out his throat. Four days he so had cried,
When Bernard hearing came to the pit's side.
"How came you thus?" he asks; he thus replied:
"Dryane am I, once noted in my city,
But nothing now save object of your pity.
Come here whoe'er you are, be merciful
And pull me out; you'll have your pockets full.
Whate'er of wealth in land or treasured hoard
Of gold I own, half shall be your reward.
And lest you doubt or to do this are loth
On all that's high in Heaven I take my oath."
Fired by the hope of gain Bernard made haste,
Into the pit a hempen rope he cast—
Which the ape seized and climbed and vanished quick.
"What imp of hell was that, what devil's trick?"
The rustic cries, " 'tis Satan's hellish spite
Has got me cozened and confounded quite.
I thought I'd help old Dryane to escape,
But bless my soul, it was that grinning ape!
'Tis no good staying here, I'll get back home,
Crossing myself lest further mischief come."

But Dryane with loud clamor multiplies
His piteous prayers: "Lest you should think" he cries
It was the devil who mocked you by his guile,
I'll recite texts and call on Saints the while.
Just throw the rope again into this cave,
And don't forget the money you're to have."
Once more to love of gold he yields; the rope
He flings, only once more to lose his hope.
Up whizzed a deadly snake of aspect grim,
And disappeared like smoke across the brim.
"Confound your gold" said Bernard, "I've no use
For it at all! Go, Dryane, to the deuce
And take your gold too! This accursed spot
Produces monsters, imps and devils hot
From hell!" He started off in flight, as though
No more returning, yet not far could go
But greed and love of gain and Dryane's gold
In ceaseless clamor promised made him hold.
Just as before, ere Dryane scarce could view it
Or grasp it with quick hand when down he threw it,
The lion seized the rope, climbed up and quit,
Leaving the man deserted in the pit.
Seeing the lion's face the rustic quailed,
His limbs shook, and with fear his visage paled.
Yet flight seemed dangerous, and a equal choice
To stay there or uplift a frightened voice;
For if he flees, then starved by long delay,
The roaring lion's prowling for his prey;
If he remains, the place is full of devils,
And daylight gone, night will bring yet more evils.
He faints, he fails, fear drains his limbs of vigour;
When spirit fails, then limbs must lose their rigour.
He's frightened more, still hearing the lament
Of Dryane wailing in abandonment,
Vouchsafing lands and wealth and castles high,

All that or tongue or mind could promise—ay,
So much he'd promised that still labouring
Both voice and breath soon failed his promising.
And had not Bernard been drawn on by greed
More than by kindness to the kindly deed,
Both lips and voice had now "tu autem" said,
And the last farewell to poor Dryane paid.
But greed all-daring that o'er perils leaps
Controls his wishes and turns back his steps.
Hunger and panting thirst burn hot for gain,
And burn more hotly when his hope proves vain.
He flung the rope, and had raised up ere then
The piteous burden from its noisesome den,
But (since in chances—evil most of all—
Varieties of issue may befall)
Just when emerging from the aperture
Even now in joy he's treading earth's firm floor,
The rope breaks! he once more to the bottom must
Have fall'n, had Bernard not with sudden thrust
Of hand caught hold and checked him falling, then
Hauled him right out and given him life again.
From death and ruin saved Cremona's lord
Was thus to country, home and lands restored.

Then Bernard made petition and besought
That he his solemn promise should make good,
But seeing him changed of aspect, all he wrought
He doth recall and how the bargain stood.
If all he cannot, let him give a portion
As suits him—but Dryane the bond outright
Denied, called Bernard mad and gave him caution
He'd call the dogs to chase him from his sight.
And the more closely shuts his mouth by threat
Against his wretched life. Then he in haste
Betakes him home, while fear his heart doth fret,

126

His finger on his lips for silence placed.
Power should be feared, 'tis sensitive to touch,

A rich man's wrath doth oft to madness rise.
Silence is safer, harping overmuch
On a lord's promise doth antagonize.
For when suspicion falls on reticence,
Words then must even more suspicion move.
There's peril when a rich man takes offence;
Trust not the rich, and hold in fear their love.
So pondered Bernard. Then on the fourth day,
When he with Burnel to the woods had gone,
By head and paw the lion made display
Beckoning, unwonted gentleness put on.
And thus he recompensed the service kind
By means within his power: the choicest meat
And tastiest parts of venison he could find
He laid before his benefactor's feet.
Ere yet the lion returned the monkey came
With look submissive, and a heap of wood
Upon his back, requiting thus the same
Help given, and showed him in the neighbourhood
A pile of seasoned logs which he had made
For him to take from. Every day he found,
All ready, flesh and firewood, tribute paid,
Whene'er he labouring trod the woodland's ground.
Nor vain the serpent's toil; in smallest size
A mighty gift he gave, for drawing near
Humbly, with gratefulness expressed in eyes
As though he fain would speak, a jewel clear
Borne in his mouth he set in Bernard's hand;
And, lest by tarrying fear should prove undoing
Of his gift's value, went and made no stand,
And so enhanced its favour by his going.
For when a giver's presence finds no favour,
Words have no place, and gifts possess no savour.
Then Bernard in amaze considering
Their gifts of wood and meat and precious stone,

Reflects, if beasts can show such valuing,
In generous, kindly gift, of service done,
How they indict the unthinking of mankind,
Ungrateful and indifferent to good.
Thus serpent, lion and monkey, to his mind,
Accuse Dryane of base ingratitude.
With gifts so precious dowered, straight to town,
Delight his footsteps speeding, Bernard flies.
He questions the artificers in stone,
Fain to explore his jewel's qualities.
"The gem's unknown to us," they say; "we hold
Nought of like nature here; to search is vain."
So needing money, thrice its weight in gold
He takes in payment, then hies home again.
Counting his money, there he finds the stone!
He'd keep it for himself, yet doth he fear
The man who bought it, one to him well known,
A courtier he, the prince's minister.
Quick to the man he will again restore
His purchased jewel (fear lends honesty)
Making excuse of error—but once more
Returned once more he there the gem doth see.
So oft he tries so often unbeheld
The gem returns; till rumour going round
Of its mysterious journeyings uncompelled
Entrance at last to royal ears hath found.
Fired by the novelty the monarch calls
A Council, summons Bernard and the rest
To tell their tale—the folk in the wide halls
Both rich and poor assembling are compressed—
Commanding, in Christ's name, by Whom he's bound,
On pain of death or exile from the state,
That whoso knows shall set forth all the ground
And tenour of the matter, and relate
What name the jewel has, what secret power

Whence brought, where found, what hidden cause
    ordains
That though possessed it cannot for an hour
Be thus retained; if he so speak, no pains
Shall he incur, no fear. Then Bernard cried
For silence, and before the king's feet fell;
Then straightway rose, his fears all set aside,
His strength resumed, and thus his tale did tell:

"Four living things had fall'n into a pit,
Three beasts, one man; none could climb out of it,
Nor would have ever, had I not been at hand.
For it had been so well devised and planned
That whosoe'er had fallen in would stay
In pitchy darkness there, beyond a doubt
For ever, unless another pulled him out.
Alone but for my donkey, then, that day
I'd gone into the forest when I heard
A piteous cry; I followed undeterred
By danger, reached the spot from whence it came,
Then made inquiry and was told the same
Was Dryane's voice, who four full days had been
There in the pit; where too had fallen in
A lion, snake and monkey, and then he
Had made a fourth in their society.
But of those three he said no word lest I
Take myself off in fright. But by and by
I learnt the truth to my great pain and cost.
Meantime Dryane by deadly terror tost
Besought my aid, then uttered threats, then vowed
To give me rich reward, and swore aloud
By all the heavenly powers, by Christ His head
And feet, by his own baptism, and the names
Of Saints, St. Thomas Cantuar and St. James,
Whose shrines he'd visit barefoot, so he said.

He promised wealth and lands, nay, all he had,
To share, if I could save him. Love of gold
Persuaded me and hope of wealth untold
To show him pity; ay, 'twas pity felt,
God be my witness, pity that did melt
My heart, his bitter moanings and his plight,
More than the gold wherewith he would requite
My toils. By these and by my skill of hand
What happened then you need not now demand;
The facts are known. That monkey, lion, snake
Live still, not I but Dryane is the cause.
For, but for him, what prayer or prize should make
Me work their safety? Four from the pit's jaws
I pulled: him last, unwilling from the first
To join them: slow he came, and why so late?
'Twas not my slowness, but his ponderous weight.
Heavy he was: would he'd been heavier yet!
Ay, would the fastenings of my rope had burst,
And all my toils been wasted! Then the pit
Had closed upon a rogue, and, as was right,
He would have lived his days in endless night.
But the three beasts to me due reverence show,
And far beyond my deeds their presents go.
Each day the lion brings me flesh to eat
From his own killing, ready ere we meet.
The monkey gathers wood, all safely stored,
For my brief service a secure reward;
And hence I take as much as I desire,
And whensoe'er I need it, for my fire.
From the snake's mouth this jewel I did take,
Whereof this Court doth inquisition make;
But whether other virtue in it rest
Than this, that none can keep it once possessed,
'Fore God, I know not. Such then, my lord king,
Such is the truth, and all this happening

131

Is as your servant has declared to you,
Not otherwise. Inquiry now pursue,
I beg, without me, and investigate
The sequence of events I here narrate.
If these my words are true I claim reward,
If false, then take my life by cross or sword."
The king then summons Dryane to the assize;
He comes as ordered, but the charge denies.
But since in the king's mind the facts stood sure,
And three in witness made the charge secure,
The prince ordains that Dryane should agree
To share with Bernard all his property,
Or else pass three days' sojurn in the pit
With those same three whom first he found in it.
The prince's judgment all the Court doth please,
And Bernard most of all! Dryane agrees
To halve his wealth and make his promise good,
Rather than trust the hazards of the wood,
Whereby he would have nought but lose the whole.
So of his wealth in misery of soul
He makes partition, but incurs no less
The name and brand of base ungratefulness.

In a short Epilogue, Nigel points the moral of the story, that ingratitude often meets with retribution, and it is better to pay willingly for services rendered than to be grudging of reward. It is also morally right, and according to God's command that whoever has done a service deserves to be rewarded, and that whoever withholds what is right incurs the risk of loss to himself. He would have the adventure of Burnel be an example to all, and recommends the reader to ponder the inward rather than the outward significance of the tale, so that he can avoid such dangers in his own case. For there are some who spend nights and days in ambitious projects, the only result of which is sudden and disastrous failure. None can strive against Nature or the lot that is appointed for him. Let Burnel be a witness, who for all his foolish strivings yet in the end remained what he was in the first. Happy he who learns caution from the dangers that beset others. Now, says Nigel, if the reader find aught in my poem that is amiss, let him correct it, commending me therewith, as should be the prayer of every man, to Mary's blessed Son.

EXPLANATORY NOTES

p. xvi   I print here the beginning only of the Letter to William, in which Nigel explains the title of the work. The rest consists of an explanation, at considerable length, of the incidents related and their allegorical interpretation. For instance, the Ass "wishes to have his tail torn out and a new one engrafted on him, because that life of the cloister, wherein he ought to endure unto the end that he may be saved, is become wholly distasteful, and he seeketh by every means how he may be torn therefrom and transplanted where a new and lengthy tail may grow unto him, that is to say, that he might be able to get unto himself a priory or an abbacy, where he can first implant a plenteous following of his own kinsmen, and thereafter draw it boastfully like a tail behind him whithersoever he goeth." Or again, "So then the Ass, who proceeds to buy useless things and stores them in glass vessels, is the monk who that he may attain the vanity which he desireth runneth about seeking the favour of men which is fragile as glass, and now allures it by flatteries, now binds it fast by gifts, and for all his labours and anxieties is advantaged not a whit, for that at far less cost could have won for himself the Kingdom of Heaven."

There can be little doubt that the William of this letter and of the verse Prologue is William de Longchamp, who at the time of the poem's composition (1179-1180) was little known and probably occupied in ingratiating himself with Richard, younger

134

son of Henry II, but who when Richard succeeded his father on the throne became Bishop of Ely and Justiciar, and subsequently Chancellor; as such, he was the recipient of the long treatise addressed to him by Nigel on the subject of misgovernment in the Church.

p. 1 Cato: supposed author of the *Distichs,* a set of maxims in verse; typical, in Medieval writings, of wisdom, as Cicero of eloquence and Ulysses of ready speech. Nestor is the aged counsellor of Homer's Iliad.

p. 3 Galen: or, as N. calls him, Galienus, was the famous Greek physician (2nd cent.). Here for any doctor.

p. 6 Louis VII, King of France (1137 to 1180).
The story comes ultimately from the Northern fable of how the bear lost part of his tail from using it to fish in the ice.

p. 11 That day: N. is very fond of this kind of repetition. He is here parodying the "Dies irae, dies illa."

p. 21 Salerno: like Montpellier, was a great medical centre in the Middle Ages.

p. 21 Luce: a pike.

p. 22 Peacock: until its tail is fully grown the peacock does not utter its cry.
Mount of Jove: the great St. Bernard Pass, so-called from a Roman temple of Jupiter.
foreign phrase: N. seems to mean that he spoke in Greek, which the ass pretends to understand.

p. 24 St. Julian: the Hospitaller, patron saint of travellers.
London merchant: there were close relations between England and (particularly Southern) Italy and Sicily, and English merchants are found at this time in many places in the Mediterranean area. Gilbert Foliot was Bishop of London, 1163 to 1189; apparently he was snub-nosed. The names in the original

are Truffator and Truffa (merchant and wife), Gila and Gula (mother and daughter), the latter two suggesting the word for unrestrained appetite (gula).

p. 28 N. seems to forget that Cremona was the home of Burnel, when he makes him travel near Lyons *before* his decision to seek Paris. One of the White Brothers: a Cistercian lay-brother employed in looking after the monastery farm. N. is here venting his intense dislike of the Cistercians.

p. 31 Punishments to be inflicted on the Cistercians: (i) tithes had been remitted on the product of their own labour, but this privilege had recently been questioned at the Lateran Council (1179); it was a serious matter as they had large estates; (ii) breeches: I use this word, with "breeks" and "drawers" for the undergarments which were the subject of a standing joke against this Order, that they followed strictly the Benedictine Rule laying down that drawers should not be worn except on journeys.

p. 32 the sack: the ancient punishment for parricide, to be drowned in a sack together with the (parricide) viper and the (infanticide) ape; Fromund had offended against the Holy Father's representative.

p. 35 Burnel's chant parodies Sedulius's Paschal Hymn, very well known in the Middle Ages, both beginning "Cantemus socii." In it he may be said to manifest what Apuleius calls "perfect asininity." We hope the translation does it full justice!

p. 39 Bologna was the great centre of legal studies (Decreta, i.e. Canon Law), as Paris was of theology (Sacred Page) and the Arts (in the academic sense).

p. 41 Apulia: William the Bad was king from 1154 to 1166. married priest: The attempt made by Gregory VII to enforce clerical celibacy was not wholly successful, and there were various ways of avoiding it.

Episcopal dispensation was necessary to the ordination of a priest's son. The "merits" of SS. Rufinus and Albinus, i.e. red gold and white silver, was a medieval joke for bribery.

p. 42 Carabella: there is a river Carapella that flows into the gulf of Manfredonia.

p. 45 The Introit for the 20th Sunday after Pentecost in the Roman Liturgy.

p. 49 Let others warfare make: originally from Ovid; adapted later to satirize the dynastic marriages of the Hapsburgs, "Let others war: thou, happy Austria, wed!"

p. 50 Paris: What subsequently became the University of Paris grew out of three schools, of the Cathedral, of the Churches of S. Geneviéve and S. Victor. The so-called Nations are not heard of before the 13th century, but there were no doubt communities of students of the same nationality in the 12th, when students in large numbers flocked to the Paris schools. "University" originally denoted the Society of Masters; there was not much difference of age, perhaps, between Masters and students, especially as the latter often remained there many years; one is quoted as having stayed there 28 years.

Wassail: Anglo-Saxon for "May there be health!" passion: seems to allude to the supposed healing effects of sexual intercourse, a belief strongly held in the M.A. The following lines play on the medieval joke against the English, that they had tails, though perhaps originally referring to pigtails. Association with them might give B. what he wanted; he seems to hint that they were concerned with tails "ante" while he was interested in tails "retro."

p. 53 So Geoffrey de Vinsauf (13th c.) calls the English drinkers and the Normans boasters, and elsewhere calls England subtle, Germany obtuse, France effeminate, Normandy boastful.

p. 55 the mitre: The episcopal mitre (described as having "horns") was taller than that of abbots. B. affects to despise abbots and their mitres as inferior, since abbots have no consecrating power, as bishops have. Hence they are "sterile" and cannot, as it were, reproduce their kind. Horns are symbolic of power.

p. 57 Simon: The sin of simony, or obtaining spiritual authority by purchase.

p. 58 Let him count as gain, etc. cf. Victor Hugo, les Misérables, Book 2, Ch. 12, the incident of Bishop Myriel and the candlesticks.

p. 63 St. Leonard: patron saint of prisoners; he lived in the 6th century while Clovis was King of the Franks. Mount of Jove; B. thinks he is looking down on Rome from the St. Bernard Pass (unless N. is using the phrase quite differently to mean the Capitol, as part of what B. is looking at). The inn, which B. reaches after 12 days, is perhaps the famous hospice of the St. Bernard. It remains the scene of subsequent action of the poem.

p. 69 Many Orders: I amend here brief particulars of the Orders mentioned. The *Knights Templars* were founded in 1118 as a religious Order for the protection of pilgrims to the Holy Land. They were so called from a palace near the Temple at Jerusalem appointed for their use. Honorius II (1124 to 1130) gave them the right to wear a white coat over the coat of mail, and Eugenius III (1145 to 1153) added a red cross. They suffered great slaughter at the battle of Jacob's Ford against Saladin in 1179.

There was a rule against galloping on horseback, but it seems to have applied to the Hospitallers and not to the Templars. The Order of *Hospitallers,* named from the Hospital of St. John the Baptist at Jerusalem, was founded for the care of sick pilgrims, but became military under Raymond de Puy 1118 to 1159). They wore a black robe with a white cross, and were austere in their living. N. accuses them of boastfulness. *Cluny* was founded in 910 for stricter observance of St. Benedict's Rule. The elaborate rendering of the offices was characteristic of them; at night one of the monks went along the seats with a lamp, to wake up any who were asleep. "Outside places" may mean subordinate posts such as dean of a grange, chamberlain, etc. "A cloud": any trouble between the brethren is checked by the abbot; he is playing here on the idea of Head and Body (see p. 73). The *Cistercians,* founded at Cîteaux in Burgundy in 1098, expanded fast, and became great landowners and rich sheep-farmers; they were rivals of and unpopular with, both Benedictines and Cluniacs. "We're here": an illusion to the story of St. Edmund's head, which after being cut off cried "Here, here" to those who were searching for it. I have omitted a number of lines in which N. discusses the question of drawers or no drawers. The Order of *Grammont,* in the diocese of Limoges, was founded in 1076, but was not transferred there till 1125. N. refers to the schism between monks and lay-brothers in 1185, in which Henry II supported the latter, King Philippe Auguste the former; the reference to there being no silences kept is perhaps ironical, as they were supposed to observe them. *Carthusians:* founded by St. Bruno in 1086, their austerities included total abstinence from meat, solitary cell (with three rooms, for eating, sleeping and praying), and goat's-hair shirt. *Augustinians,* not monks, but clergy living according to Rule (so-called) of St. Augustine, based on advice found in his writings; they wore a black cassock over a white linen surplice. Order of *Prémontré* (near Laon): regular canons founded in 1120 by St. Norbert, but wearing only white, and more ascetic. *Secular Canons* were secular clergy, attached to a cathedral or large church, living a common life but without any rule; this would seem to monks to allow overmuch license, but N.'s special cause of dislike probably was that the Canterbury monks were at this time threatened with expulsion and replacement by Secular Canons. *Nunneries:* Nigel probably had in mind the recent scandal of the Amesbury Nuns, whose Abbess was supposed to have had three children. The Order of *Sempringham* (consistently mis-spelt by N.) was the only order of English origin, having been founded by St. Gilbert in 1148; the men were to be Augustinian Canons, the women Benedictine Nuns; the wall in the church was to be high enough to prevent men and women seeing one another; it was 5 feet thick.

Gerald of Wales tells a story of how one of the nuns fell in love with St. Gilbert (Gemma Eccl. 2.17).

A later and more scurrilous parallel to B.'s new order is "The Order of Fair Ease" (Camden Soc. 1839, p. 137) in the reign of Edward I.

p. 85 tail behind: After this line N. plays on the Latin words "capio" (take) and "caput" (head), and then for another four lines on the conjugation of the word "take," past, present and future.

p. 87 taking flesh of beasts: Attacks on the game-laws were common among writers of the time in England. Forests were the personal property of the kings, who strictly controlled the hunting rights.

gifts: the implied meaning is, of course, bribes, but I have preferred to keep the other word. N. probably had in mind, e.g. Psalm 15.6, 26-10 (P.B. Version).

p. 93 while yet the baby: Bestowal of the offices of the church on children was dealt with by a canon of the Lateran Council of 1179; nobody was to be appointed bishop under the age of 30, or dean, archdeacon, etc., under 25.

p. 94 a perch: The words used by N. are "esox" (devourer) and "lupus" (wolf), both commonly used for "pike." I have ventured to substitute "perch" for the latter. After the following couplet he has one more of his excruciating puns: the "canine" bayings are dearer than the "canonical" chantings.

> Perhaps if I might go one better than Nigel,
> Dogs please him more than dogmas, one
>   and all,
> And canine bark more than notes canonical.

p. 95 Bernard: The reference is to St. Bernard (1090 to 1153), the founder of the famous Cistercian monastery at Clairvaux.

p. 96 The wolf: The point is that the animals are apparently harmless, but really dangerous.

p. 98 I heard a sound of chattering: Chaucer may have had these lines of Nigel in mind, cf. Parliament of Fowls 312-5:

> And so huge a noyse gan they make
> That erthe and eyr and tre and every lake
> So ful was, that unnethé was there space
> For me to stonde, so ful was al the place.

p. 102 Be warned by me: Between this and the preceding stanza there are, in the original, thirty lines, in which the raven speaks his views on Confessors. I have omitted them since (i) the raven speaks entirely out of character, which is not the case elsewhere with him or with the other birds, (ii) the lines add considerably to the length of his speech, which, as the

141

Cock thinks, is excessive! (iii) most of the lines are in the form of couplets beginning with the same phrase (favourite with N., as we have seen on p. 18f), and so unsuitable for translation into stanza form. After complaining that he risks death whether he speaks or keeps silent, the raven accuses priests of telling what they have heard in the confessional: "The babbling tongues of priests who reveal secrets cause us to be unwilling to confess; no worse plague is there than one who reveals what he has been told in confidence." He goes on to depict the character of the righteous priest (it may be suggested that N. is taking this opportunity to add his picture of the ideal father confessor to that of the ideal bishop which Burnel gives us earlier on). If such a one were found anywhere in the world, to such a confessor, says the raven, he would willingly confess all. The raven's guilt consisted in (i) not returning to Noah in the Ark, (ii) in revealing to Apollo the unfaithfulness of Coronis, a maiden whom he loved. For this he was turned from white to black, a punishment related in both Hebrew and Classical mythology.

p. 108   Asthma and falling sickness: (see p. 50 above). In the preceding stanza he refers to an abortion secretly performed.

p. 114   Stygian stream: i.e. she had been a goddess.

p. 117   the new moon: she refers to the crescent-shaped space revealed on the girl's bare buttocks, as she lifts up her skirt behind.

Three Sisters: the legend is much the same as that of the three Norns of Scandinavian folk-lore, who give rewards and punishments, and distribute riches and prosperity. As in this version, they do not always agree.

142

p. 122 The story of the Grateful Beasts is found in the Sanskrit collection of apologues called Panchatantra, in *Kalila and Dimna,* an Arabian version, and in various other places. It is also told by the chronicler Matthew Paris under the year 1195, as a favourite tale of Richard I, used by him to rebuke the ingratitude of English barons and stir them up to take arms for the Holy Land. In this form the rich man is named Vitalis, and the peasant is a charcoal-burner.